Other books by Janet and Alex D'Amato

American Indian Craft Inspirations
Gifts to Make for Love or Money
African Crafts for You to Make
Colonial Crafts for You to Make
African Animals Through African Eyes
Handicrafts for Holidays
Indian Crafts
Cardboard Carpentry

Quillwork

THE CRAFT OF PAPER FILIGREE

JANET and ALEX D'AMATO

M. EVANS AND COMPANY, INC.
New York, N. Y. 10017

M. Evans and Company titles are distributed in
the United States by the J. B. Lippincott Company,
East Washington Square, Philadelphia, Pa. 19105;
and in Canada by McClelland & Stewart Ltd.,
25 Hollinger Road, Toronto M4B 3G2, Ontario

Library of Congress Cataloging in Publication Data

D'Amato, Janet.
    Quillwork, the craft of paper filigree.

    Includes index.
    1. Paper quillwork. I. D'Amato, Alex, joint
author. II. Title.
TT870.D26 1975   745.54   74-26757
ISBN 0-87131-171-2
ISBN 0-87131-177-1 pbk.

I. Quilling.

Design by Alex D'Amato

Manufactured in the United States of America

9 8 7 6 5 4 3 2 1

On the title page is a colonial looking-glass. The frame (about 17½" x 14") is divided into eight sections. Side sections show quillwork baskets of flowers and triple-tiered fountains. In the top section there is a quilled castle with glass birds, jester and dog. A blonde wax figure stands in the doorway. In bottom section are shells and mica with quillwork trees on either side.

Contents&

PICTURE CREDITS

We are grateful to these museums for permission to
reproduce the following photographs:
Mirror frames, pages 3, 12, 13, and 124,
SHELBURNE MUSEUM, INC., Shelburne, Vermont;
sconce, page 11, courtesy of the COOPER-HEWITT MUSEUM
OF DECORATIVE ARTS AND DESIGN, Smithsonian Institution;
hatchment, page 7, THE METROPOLITAN
MUSEUM OF ART, Rogers Fund, 1938; spoon,
page 118, THE METROPOLITAN MUSEUM OF
ART, gift of Mrs. S. P. Avery, 1897; birdcage,
page 119, and sled (shown here with front runners
cropped slightly), page 120, THE METROPOLITAN
MUSEUM OF ART, gifts of Mrs. Morris Falman
in the name of her late husband; card case, page
120, THE METROPOLITAN MUSEUM OF ART,
gift of Mrs. Amelia Lazarus in the name of Emilia
Lazarus, 1895; sconce, page 123, THE METROPOLITAN
MUSEUM OF ART, gift of Mrs. J. Insley Blair, 1948.
Cover photograph by Stanley Patz.
All other photographs by Frank Stork.

*The hatchment (Dering coat of arms), shown
on the opposite page, was made by Eunice
Deering and features four mosaic coiled deers'
heads. Red and gold motifs are placed against
a blue-green background, and the date, 1731,
is quilled at the bottom.*

Quillwork

THE CRAFT OF PAPER FILIGREE

An example of seventeenth century European quillwork, this heraldic piece has a shield framed with delicate scrollwork.

History & Introduction

The spiral and other curves occur often in nature: a fern frond uncurling, a seed pattern, the sea shell. Throughout the world nature's "spirals" have been re-created by artists—painted, etched and carved in stone or ivory, shaped in gold and silver. Over the centuries, spiral-inspired designs developed into the ornate intricacy called "filigree." By the thirteenth and fourteenth centuries tiny medallions to great cathedrals were adorned with elaborate filigree art.

Quillwork, the art of "paper filigree" was a paper imitation of the precious-metal filigree. Basically, quilling is the craft of curling a narrow strip of paper around a thin shaft, then gluing the scroll or spiral edge to a background. Since a bird feather (quill) without the feathering was used as the shaft, the craft of "rolled paperwork" was called "quilling." When coils were varied in shape and clustered, intricate designs were created. Painted gold, a quilled design appeared to be golden metal filigree; in white, it had the look of finely carved ivory.

Possibly as far back as the thirteenth or fourteenth century, perhaps somewhere in a European convent, a nun curled a strip of paper and appreciated its possibilities. It could have happened when the Bible pages that had been hand decorated were trimmed and mounted. These paper trimmings were put aside since paper was never discarded. Narrow, thin strips—what could be done with them? Some unknown person found that by curling and gilding them, they created the gold filigree look so desired and admired for framing religious medallions and pictures sent to them by the pope. This inexpensive way to create filigree filled a great need of those times since the devoted members of the Church felt symbols of the faith should be embellished as lavishly as possible.

It is known that by the seventeenth century Italian nuns skilled in this craft made various religious items, frames, and crosses of paper coils. The art spread to France and Spain, where again it was mostly used for religious articles.

Paper for quilling was often painted in colors or edges of strips were painted gold. Seventeenth century books usually had gilded page edges. A discarded book was a source of precious paper, especially the edges. It is rumored that numerous seventeenth century manuscripts and books had their pages trimmed ⅛″ shorter than usual to provide gilded edge strips for zealous quillers.

In England early paper rolling was devoted to religious articles. But by the late seventeenth century it became a fad among English ladies of fashion, and by 1700 tutors were available to teach the craft. The English ladies covered tea caddies and vanity boxes, surrounded needlework or painted or wax portraits with quilled borders, did heraldic pieces, and even covered furniture. One cabinet still in existence was covered with a mosaic of paper coils, 135 coils to the square inch. There is a record of an order to deliver filigree paper to the daughter of King George III. A magazine article of 1786 gives instructions and notes for quilling, indicating that any amateur could make paper filigree. Patterns were given to make a design for a box top and other ornaments.

Quite naturally, this craft was brought from England to the colonies, and it became very popular in America during the eighteenth century. Fine examples can be seen today in museums featuring colonial exhibits. American quilling developed its own character and vitality.

Among the most notable examples of American quillwork were the sconces. Flowers were included in these quilled compositions, their petals covered with mica flakes and edged with wire coils. Placed in a deep shadow box with a candle bracket, the quilling was covered with glass. When the candle was lit, it must have produced a delightful effect, reflecting on the mica chips. As there are many similar sconces (most from Massachusetts) it is possible that some were done by professional craftsmen to meet a demand.

Other American quilled pieces included framed designs, edgings for portraits, and mirror frames. Many colonial schoolgirls learned quilling as part of their education. An advertisement in a Boston paper of 1775 stated that the many crafts taught

This fine colonial sconce dates about 1720. The deep frame, painted black and covered with glass, has a silver bracket attached to hold the candle. Within the frame is the quill-work design of scrolls and pointed coils. Wire edged flowers—roses, tulips, carnations and others—fill the center above the quilled vase.

by a Mrs. Hiller included filigree and quillwork. Ladies such as Eunice Deering and Mary Jamison became known for their quilling skill.

Quilled pieces had various looks. On some, large open areas contrasted with edges and medallions of scrolls and volutes. Paper mosaics were made of tight coils of various colors that covered the entire surface. Some pieces had multilayers of

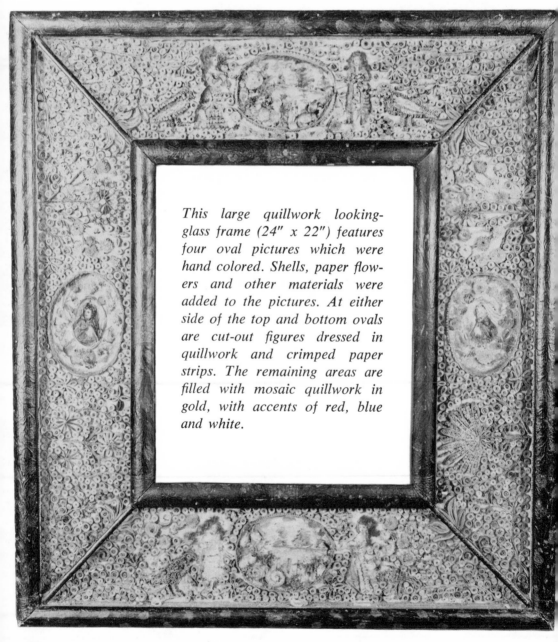

This large quillwork looking-glass frame (24" x 22") features four oval pictures which were hand colored. Shells, paper flowers and other materials were added to the pictures. At either side of the top and bottom ovals are cut-out figures dressed in quillwork and crimped paper strips. The remaining areas are filled with mosaic quillwork in gold, with accents of red, blue and white.

quilling. Many were collages of various elements combined with the quilling: printed or painted medallions, wax figures, wire, pinecones, burrs, shells, silk threads, feathers, and beads, as well as the mica chips.

The popularity of quilling died out soon after the beginning of the nineteenth century. Briefly revived in the Victorian era, it is a long neglected craft. Recently it has become popular again —possibly because of the interest today in nostalgia and hand-craftsmanship. Quilling, although primarily ornamental, is no less practical today than it was two hundred years ago. Many examples of colonial quillwork are now museum pieces, valuable as fine art. Quilling created today could be next century's heirloom, and now we have improved materials—colored papers, plastics, excellent transparent glues, and spray paints.

To create your own quilling, all you need to do is to learn the basic coils, rolls, and scrolls. With practice, no project will be too complex. Some of the projects suggested in this book are quite simple. Others take considerable time (and keep your hands busy while you are watching TV). Many crafts such as needlepoint or applying sequins to ornaments take considerable time, yet the time or units used to create the work of art are rarely counted—it is the enjoyment and final effect that are important. So, too, with quilling: some projects use many coils and are intended to take time to create something that will be greatly admired. This book suggests all sorts of quillwork, from open delicate pieces to the solidly filled mosaics. Many are inspired by antique pieces; others are contemporary, modern quilling.

This is a corner detail (a 4½" square area) of the mirror frame shown on the title page. A grotto scene with shells, coral, and a small figure sprinkled with ground-up irridescent shells, is surrounded by quillwork scrolls and fluting (crimping).

Materials & Methods

Of all crafts, quilling can be one of the least expensive for the elegant results obtained. You probably have most of the materials around the house right now to set up a convenient area for making even the most intricate quilling (fig. 1).

A. Hatpin: the most essential and convenient tool for rolling the paper strips (your "quill"). A round toothpick may also be used.
B. Paper strips (see next page).
C. Quilling board: a piece of corrugated cardboard about 8" x 10" with waxed paper taped around it. You can slip patterns under the paper, and glue the quilling together on top. As glue does not adhere to waxed paper, the completed design can be lifted off. Change the waxed paper frequently, since it gets full of holes and glue.
D. Straight pins or corsage pins: pushed through the rolls into the corrugated board while gluing, these help hold the coils in position.
E. White glue (see page 17).
F. Pencil, paper, and ruler: to draw patterns and plan designs. Use thin tracing paper (available in art stores) to trace designs from the book. Place the designs under the waxed paper.
G. Large scissors: for cutting the paper strips.
H. Small scissors: for snipping short lengths of strips, these are less tiring than large scissors.

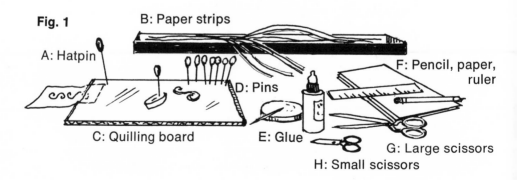

Fig. 1
A: Hatpin
B: Paper strips
C: Quilling board
D: Pins
E: Glue
F: Pencil, paper, ruler
G: Large scissors
H: Small scissors

PAPER FOR QUILLING: Almost any reasonably sturdy paper can be used: construction paper, heavy typewriter paper, bond, Strathmore. It must be thin enough to curl, yet sturdy and resilient enough to hold its shape and form graceful curls. Experiment with various papers by cutting and rolling strips ⅛″ to ¼″ wide.

Some papers are inclined to curl more than others. With some that do not curl easily, dampen the tip before coiling. Most strips will curl without dampening. More stubborn types of paper may need the entire strip dampened slightly. Use a damp sponge. A good sense of touch is the only way to determine what is needed. Discard those papers that prove to be too thick or stiff or become too limp.

It is also possible to use up old paper, even printed matter (how about all that junk mail?); you can spray-paint quilling made with printed papers. Calendar sheets are often a good weight. If you are buying paper for quilling, ask for single ply or about 70-pound text.

To make smooth curves, you must cut the strips of paper *with* the grain. Cut one strip from the side and another strip from the end of a piece of paper. Roll each. One direction usually will curl more easily and smoothly than the other (fig. 2).

Cut the paper with large scissors, two or three thicknesses at a time. Scissor cutting gives a "handmade" look for an antique piece. The slight variations of widths keep the unit from looking machine-made. Or you can cut the paper with a single edged razor blade in a holder, or an X-acto knife (fig. 3), using a metal-edged ruler as a guide. In a few minutes, you can cut enough strips for hours of quilling. Keep the cut strips in a box (such as a candle box). Most patterns use ⅛″ strips; some use ¼″

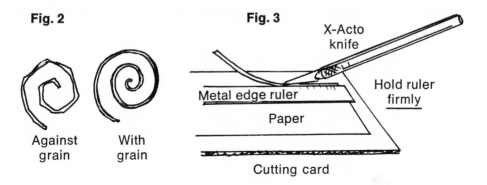

Fig. 2

Against grain   With grain

Fig. 3

X-Acto knife

Metal edge ruler

Hold ruler firmly

Paper

Cutting card

or ⅜" strips, which are easier to handle for certain larger designs and for children's projects. Strips can be cut of colored paper or white paper can be painted with water colors for delicate color effects.

Precut paper quilling strips in many attractive colors are available from craft suppliers (see page 125). Usually ⅛" wide (depending on the supplier), the strips are quite long (about 22" to 26") and may tend to tangle even though they are glued together at one end. It's best to keep them in a long box such as a florist's box for long-stemmed roses or a box that contained gift-wrapping paper. Remove the strips from the attached rather than the loose end.

To my knowledge, there is no gold or silver paper suitable for quilling, yet the effects of gold and silver are very desirable. After the quilling is made, you can spray it lightly with gold or silver spray-can paint. Be careful not to have excess glue on these pieces since the glue becomes a noticeable gold lump after it is spray-painted.

Antique pieces were often made of paper with a gilt edge, which was presumably painted on. Gold edges give a more delicate effect to quilling than spraying. If you want your piece to look gilt-edged, carefully paint the top edge of each coil, using a brush and gold paint, after the quilling is finished and glued in position. This paint can be found in craft and art stores; some brands are sold for model makers. Some suppliers (see page 125) carry gilt-edged paper.

QUILLING BOARD: Corrugated board is fine for assembling most quilling, but as you create more complex units, you may want a board that you can stick pins into more easily. Buy a ½" or ¾" thick piece of Styrofoam® brand plastic foam.* Tape a small plastic ruler to one edge of the board. This saves searching for a ruler to measure the lengths to cut strips (fig. 4). Cut a piece of waxed paper, fold it around the board, and tape it in the back.

* *Trademark of the Dow Chemical Company*

16

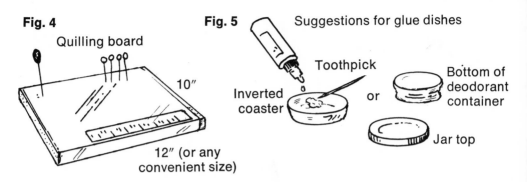

Fig. 4
Quilling board

10"

12" (or any
convenient size)

Fig. 5   Suggestions for glue dishes

Toothpick

Inverted
coaster   or

Bottom of
deodorant
container

Jar top

GLUES: Use any type of paper glue. The white glues such as Elmer's and Sobo are best since they are transparent when dry and come in handy squeeze-top bottles. Squeeze out only a drop or so at a time onto a corner of the waxed paper or onto a glass coaster (fig. 5). Get a small bottle—it is less tiring since you will be squeezing every few seconds—then refill it from a larger bottle. Apply glue to the coils with a toothpick.

Use the same glue to attach the quilling to a background. If you want to attach the quilling to fabric or plastic, check the glue labels; Sobo is excellent for fabrics.

To glue a thin sheet of paper onto a card for a background, it is better to use rubber cement (from stationery or art stores). Spread the cement on both surfaces. When the glue is almost dry, lay the surfaces together, press down and rub off any excess with your fingers.

OTHER MATERIALS:

Masking tape is helpful to tape the waxed paper in place and to tape on patterns for tracing. When pinning isn't practical, use masking tape to hold the quilled units in position while the glue dries.

Hair clips, single pronged, are useful, since they are delicate enough for holding coils while the glue dries or for holding pieces together in spots where they can't be pinned.

Tweezers can be helpful for positioning tiny units and jewels.

A damp towel is handy, because your hands and all materials must be kept very clean. White glue washes off easily with a damp towel.

Quilling Fundamentals

BASIC SHAPES

All quilling patterns, no matter how complex, are formed from just a few basic coils and scrolls with simple variations. If you practice these basics, you will soon be adept enough to do any project in this book. Many of the creations shown may look complex, but the effect is usually achieved by adding many more of the basic coils. And while these may take more time and patience, they require no more skill than the simple designs made with a few coils.

Each description of a basic coil is followed by a project for practice. You can make each practice project with ³⁄₁₆″ wide strips of construction paper (or purchased paper strips) and mount it on paper or a card. Next to the directions for each project is a diagram showing the placement of each coil, and figures indicating the length of the strip of paper used to make it. The design is shown slightly apart (fig. 1); that is, the coils are shown *not* touching so that you will be able to distinguish one coil or scroll from another. However, they should be glued together at each adjacent point. If they were shown attached (fig. 2), it might be difficult to determine the individual scrolls. Throughout the book patterns are drawn this way.

Fig. 1

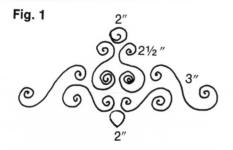

DESIGN DIAGRAM (Pattern)

Fig. 2

**ACTUAL APPEARANCE
(Glued together)**

Round Coils

Cut some practice strips about 8″ long. Lay the hatpin against one end and stroke the pin firmly along the end of the strip to the tip (somewhat like curling gift wrap ribbon). This gives the strip the inclination to curl (fig. 1). Then make a controlled winding around the hatpin, hold and guide the paper strip with the other hand. Roll toward you (fig. 2), rolling up the paper. Keep rolling, making a tight coil (fig. 3). For large coils, once you've started rolling, it is sometimes easier to remove the pin and continue rolling with your fingers. Try rolling both ways and see which is easier for you.

When a strip is completely rolled, use a toothpick to add a tiny dab of glue to the end. Hold the roll for a few seconds until the glue sets.

Fig. 1   **Fig. 2**   Roll

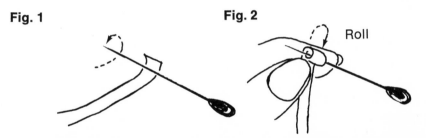

For an open round shape, roll the paper the same way, but before gluing, slightly release your hold on the coil and allow it to unroll a bit. When the coil is the proper "openness" (fig. 4), glue the end as before. Hold it with your fingers or a hair clip until the glue sets.

Fig. 3   **Tight coil**   **Fig. 4**   **Loose coil**

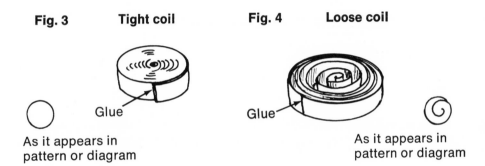

Glue

As it appears in
pattern or diagram

Glue

As it appears in
pattern or diagram

COILS: Tight   **Loose coils**

When a smooth outer contour of the roll is important in the design, tear the end of the strip rather than cutting it. As the end is glued to the roll, it blends against it (fig. 5).

When using these coils as a design filler (see the bell on page 36), gluing the ends is often not necessary, since the coils will be glued to each other and hold their shape in this manner. Some designs call for loose unglued coils (fig. 6).

Fig. 5   **Fig. 6**

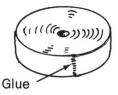

Glue

Making a quantity of coils may be repetitious, but it can be done while watching TV or chatting with friends. A shallow candy box with plastic molded separations makes a good container for the rolled coils.

CROSS SAMPLE: For a practice project, make a cross of coils. Trace the design (fig. 7) and slip it under the waxed paper. Make coils, using strips the length indicated in the diagram. Pin the coils over the tracing, and add a small dab of glue to each spot where the coils touch. Hold the design with pins set vertically in each coil (fig. 8). Repeat until all the coils are glued. When the glue is dry, remove the pins by gently twisting them out.

Lift the unit off the waxed paper. Cut a 4″ x 5″ piece of a contrasting color paper. Mark an "X" where the center of cross should be. Add dabs of glue to the backs of the coils, turn the cross over, and set it in position on the background. Press it down until the glue holds. Or set it on the board and pin through the background to hold the cross in position until the glue dries.

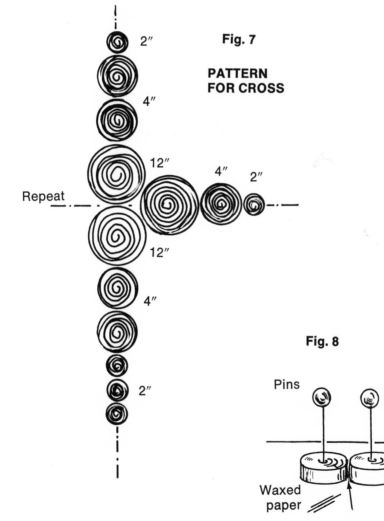

Fig. 7

**PATTERN
FOR CROSS**

2″

4″

12″

4″ 2″

Repeat

12″

4″

2″

Fig. 8

Pins

Waxed
paper

Glue

Pinched Coils

Loose coils can be made into many shapes by pinching them in various ways. Pinch one end to achieve a petal shape (fig. 1). If only the tip end is pinched, the center remains round (fig. 2). Keep the coil well between your fingers and pinch up to the middle to achieve the proper inner shape (fig. 1).

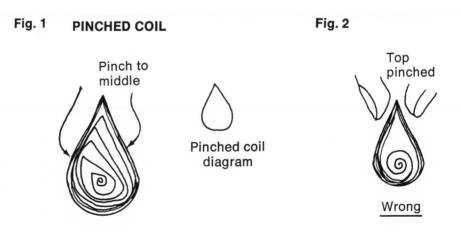

Fig. 1   **PINCHED COIL**

Pinch to middle

Pinched coil diagram

Fig. 2

Top pinched

Wrong

DOUBLE PINCHED COIL

Fig. 3

Diagram

Fig. 4   **VARIATIONS**

3 pinched
corners

4 pinched
corners

pinch
one
side,
shape
sideways

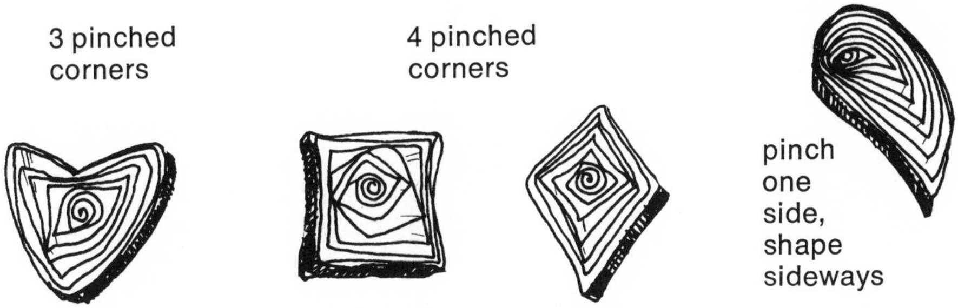

Pinch both ends for a cat's eye (fig. 3). Experiment pinching in three or four spots, or push sideways as you pinch. All sorts of useful shapes can be formed (fig. 4).

Tear the end of the strip, roll, and add glue as you pinch. It will slide a bit, but then hold, since the pinching helps push glue onto the paper.

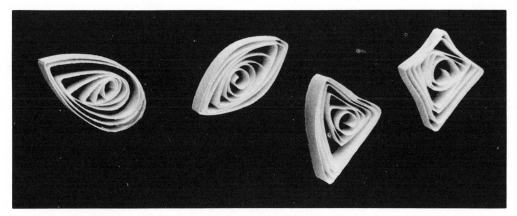

COILS: pinched

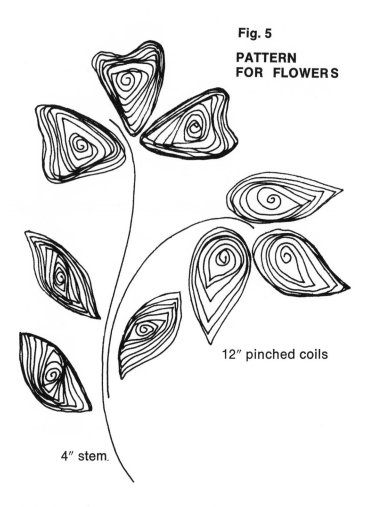

Fig. 5

PATTERN FOR FLOWERS

12″ pinched coils

4″ stem.

FLOWER SAMPLE: For a practice project, make flowers and leaves with pinched shapes. Trace the design (fig. 5), and place it under the waxed paper. Make pinched shapes in the sizes shown. With a little practice, you'll see how much to allow coil to spring open for the right size pinched coil. Leaves are double pinched coils. One flower has petals pinched at one end. For the other flower, pinch one end, then gently shape the coil by pinching it at the top corners. Glue the petals around the flower and to the ends of the stems. Glue the stems together, and then glue the leaves on. Working on the board, pin the coils wherever necessary. When the glue is dry, remove the finished piece and glue the unit into position on a 5″ x 7″ background.

Scrolls

There are endless variations of scrolls. Practice with 3½″ strips. Make a basic scroll (fig. 1), rolling *in* from each end. Scroll ends are not glued; the shape is maintained when the scrolls are glued to each other and to the background.

Fig. 1 **Fig. 2** **Fig. 3**

For an "S" scroll, roll one end of a strip halfway, remove the pin, turn the strip, and roll the other end (fig. 2). Variations can be made by curling one end more than other end (fig. 3). Practice making many scrolls, and lay them around and next to each other to see how they create a filigree look (fig. 4).

Fig. 4

SCROLL FRAME SAMPLE: For practice make an attractive frame using only scrolls. Cut a 3″ circle from a greeting card or photograph. The pattern (fig. 5) shows one-quarter of the frame. Trace the other quarters, repeating the design. Place

Fig. 5

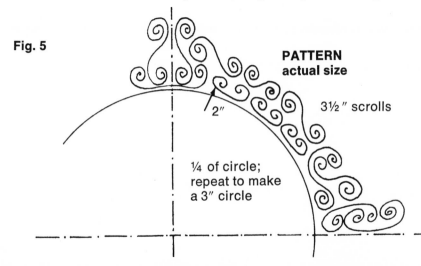

PATTERN
actual size

3½″ scrolls

2″

¼ of circle;
repeat to make
a 3″ circle

the completed frame drawing under the waxed paper. Make scrolls for the top, center, and side motifs first. Add glue at spots where the scrolls touch; pin to hold them in position until glue sets. Fill scrolls in between, stretching or condensing them as necessary to fit the picture. Scrolls need considerable pinning to hold them in position, but once glued to each other they are sturdy.

When the frame is dry, lift it off the waxed paper. Cut a 4″ x 5″ background and place it on the quilling board. Glue on the picture, then glue the quilled frame around the picture, slightly over the edge, holding it in position with pins until the glue dries. Place the finished piece in a ¼″ deep frame if desired.

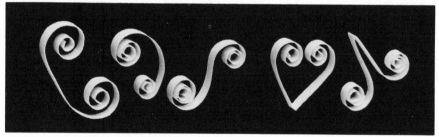

SCROLLS: "S" scrolls   Folded scrolls

Scrolls With Folds

These are really a variation of scrolls. There is no gluing until the shapes are positioned. Practice with 3½″ strips. Fold a strip in half and curl inward from both ends (fig. 1) to create a heart shape. Fold a strip in half and curl outward on both ends (fig. 2) to make a "V" shape. There are endless variations. Make the curls both to one side; or make long or short curls with the fold at a third or a quarter of the strip (fig. 3). Try your own variations.

Fig. 1   Fig. 2

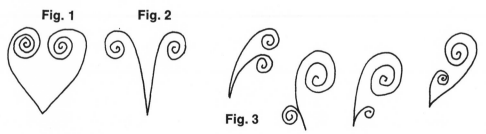

Fig. 3

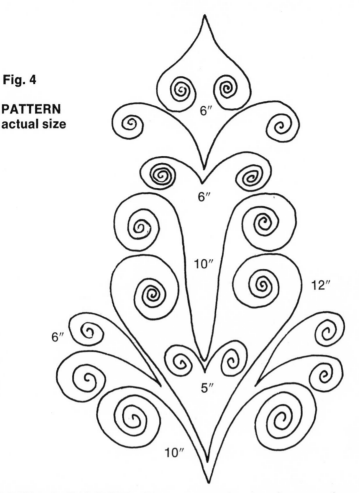

Fig. 4

PATTERN actual size

6″
6″
10″
12″
6″
5″
10″

FILIGREE SAMPLE: For a practice project, make a simple filigree unit. Trace the design (fig. 4) and place it under the waxed paper. Curl the units indicated, placing the larger units first and filling in with smaller units. Glue the units together and hold them in position with pins until the glue dries. Gently lift the design off the board. For the background, cut a 5″ x 7″ piece of paper in a contrasting color and lay it on the board. Add dabs of glue to the filigree unit. Position it on the background, and hold it with pins until the glue dries.

You have now made all the basic quilled shapes. If your coils or scrolls look somewhat different from the ones shown, they are not necessarily wrong. Paper or quilling techniques can vary. Variations sometimes look more attractive than the original.

Experiment to achieve various effects of your own. For instance, cut a strip from the deckle edge of writing paper or cut one edge of a strip with pinking shears. Use a coil of this strip as a flower center. Add layers, or overlap shapes—quilling has many possibilities.

When many filler coils or a quantity of scrolls are needed, do a few at a time and glue them in place; then see how many more will be needed. The number of coils needed on a project is not specified here, since one quiller may coil more tightly than another and so will use more coils. I find it is more interesting to make coils for a while, then glue them in position, and then roll some more, but some quillers prefer to do all the rolling before gluing.

	Tight coils	Loose coils	Pinched coils
1½″			
2″			
4″			
8″			
10″			
12″			
22″			

On some of the more intricate pieces, it may be impossible to indicate the length of the strips of all the pieces on the pattern. You will soon find, as you work, that you can judge the approximate length of strip needed to get a certain shape. An experienced quiller rarely needs to be told lengths. Below are basic charts to help beginners. Repeats should be made of strips cut to identical lengths.

Creating your own designs comes easy after a while. Lay together scrolls, rolls and pinched shapes, and ideas will form. Although many people say, "I can't draw a straight line," they don't need to. Everyone doodles, and quilling patterns are all scrolls and doodles.

	Scrolls		Folded scrolls
1½″			
2″			
3″			
5″			
7″			
12″			

ADDITIONAL SHAPES AND TECHNIQUES

For certain effects, you can use other paper forms along with the coils and scrolls. Antique pieces had enclosed shapes, crimping (pleating), lattice, conical coils, and flowers with petals covered with mica chips for glitter.

Enclosed Shapes

Enclosed shapes help define a design and make it easier to fill areas with coils. On some, the back is left open and a strip of quilling paper surrounds the coils (fig. 1). On others, the paper strip is glued to the edge of a cardboard shape creating a solid flat background (fig. 2).

To make an enclosed shape with a solid background, cut the shape desired out of a card or heavy paper. Place the shape on the waxed paper. Lay a line of glue along the edge of the card, and shape a strip with your fingers, fitting it to the curves. Hold the strip in position vertically with pins on both sides of strip, using as many as necessary. Cut off the excess at the end, and glue where the ends meet (fig. 2). When the glue is dry, remove the inner pins and fill the shape with coils or desired design.

For an open background, draw the desired shape on paper and slip it under the waxed paper. Shape the strip around it, glue the ends, and hold with pins as before. Leave the pins in place, removing them only as the inside coils are glued to each other and to the edging strip (see fig. 1). When the coils completely fill in the inside, the enclosing edge will hold its shape.

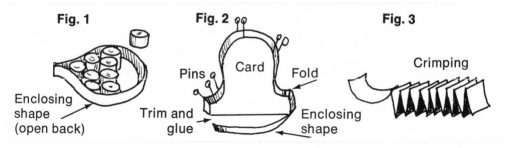

Fig. 1
Enclosing shape (open back)

Fig. 2
Pins   Card   Fold
Trim and glue   Enclosing shape

Fig. 3
Crimping

Crimping

Usually, crimping is placed in a narrow enclosed shape. Make an enclosing shape of the size needed. To make crimping, take a strip of quilling paper and accordion pleat it (fig. 3). Make the pleats slightly wider than the area to be occupied (fig. 4). Pleating cannot be exact, but keep it as uniform as possible, judging by eye. Let the pleating spring open, and check the area where it is to be placed. If more is needed, pleat another strip and glue it to the end of the first strip.

Add glue to the inside and base of the enclosing shape (fig. 5). While holding crimping together in folded form, add glue to the edge that will be attached to the base. Turn the crimping over, release it, and ease it between the sides of the shape. Space the pleats as evenly as possible with pins, adding glue and pins wherever necessary (fig. 6).

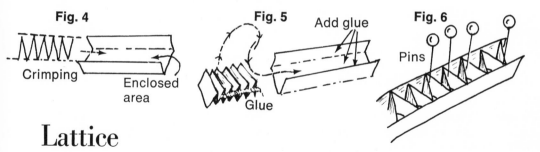

Fig. 4

Crimping

Enclosed area

Fig. 5 Add glue

Glue

Fig. 6

Pins

Lattice

Cut quilling strips narrow, less than ⅛″. Draw a pattern for the spacing desired, and place it under the waxed paper. Lay the strips on the waxed paper, and glue at each intersection, making a crisscross pattern (fig. 7). When the glue is dry, trim the ends to make the shape desired, and add an enclosing edge (fig. 8).

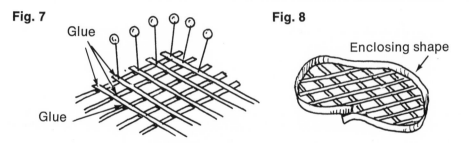

Fig. 7

Glue

Glue

Fig. 8

Enclosing shape

Flowers With Wire Edges

Interesting additions to many colonial pieces were flowers that appear to have been cut of some sort of paper or card or shaped out of wax or papier-mâché. The petals, covered with mica chips or crushed irridescent shells, were edged with finely coiled wire (see the sconces on pages 11 and 123).

To re-create this effect, cut petal shapes (fig. 9) out of lightweight cardboard, such as the back of a writing pad or a cereal box. Bend slightly along the center line. Paint the petals the color desired, and allow to dry. As a substitute for the mica or shells, buy clear transparent or translucent glitter (available in craft stores and some dime stores). Cover the surface of the painted petal with glue, sprinkle on the glitter, and shake off the excess.

To make the wire edges, use thin beading wire of gold or silver (available in craft stores). Cut a piece about 6″ long, and wind it around the hatpin (fig. 10). Start the wire near the head of the pin, and roll the hatpin, guiding the spiral twists with your other hand (fig. 11). Slide it off, and you have a tight, tiny spiral. Pull the spiral out slightly.

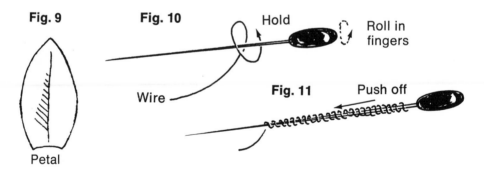

Fig. 9 **Fig. 10** Hold Roll in fingers

Wire **Fig. 11** Push off

Petal

Twist the wire ends together near the base of the petal (fig. 12), and hold them with a hair clip. Pull the spiral up around the petal, and add glue, attaching the wire to the edge of the petal (fig. 13). Hold with pins or clips until the glue dries.

When each petal is edged, assemble the flower. To make the petals stand away from the background, use a temporary

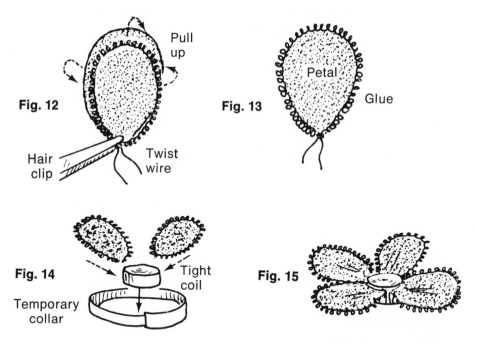

Fig. 12

Pull up

Hair clip

Twist wire

Fig. 13

Petal

Glue

Fig. 14

Temporary collar

Tight coil

Fig. 15

collar. Glue a ¼" strip of paper in a circle slightly smaller than the outside diameter of the finished flower (fig. 14). Glue the ends of the petals to a tight center coil, with the outside edges resting on the collar. When the glue is dry, remove the collar, and glue the completed flower to the background (fig. 15).

Conical Shapes

In antique quilled compositions, a pointed, conical coil was often used for a flower center, or several cones were clustered together (fig. 16).

Fig. 16   Detail of an old piece

Side view of center area

To make a conical coil, cut one end of the quilling strip at a sharp angle. Lay the hatpin against the angle (fig. 17), and roll, making a point and a tight spiral. Add dabs of glue as you go along (fig. 18). After the point is formed, continue making the coil (the pin can be removed if desired), making the base a flat coil. Add glue to keep the coil very tight (fig. 19).

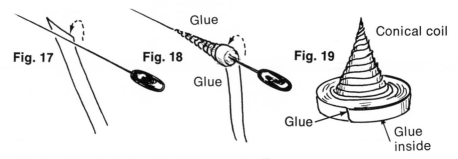

Other Added Materials

Don't be afraid to combine various materials and handwork with quilling. If you study antique pieces, you will get ideas for additions that combine well and enhance the piece. Old quilling was combined with stuffed fabrics, small figurines, hand-colored engravings, many natural materials (see page 124), and other less identifiable objects.

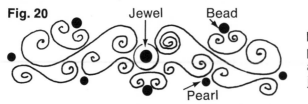

Black dots in a pattern indicate added beads or jewels

Trimmings sold in craft stores for boutique decorating enhance quilling. Some possibilities are pearls, plastic stringed beads, glue-on jewels, decorative gold cords, and gold-embossed paper edgings. Beads or jewels are usually indicated by a black dot in a pattern (fig. 20).

Throughout the book there will be suggestions for added effects such as embedding in plastic (page 74) or adding tubettini clusters (page 68).

BELL-SAMPLE PROJECT: For practice, make a bell, using added shapes and materials. For a card, this bell could be a green and gold Christmas bell or a white wedding bell or a silver anniversary one. For a first anniversary (paper), quilling makes an especially appropriate remembrance.

Trace the outside edge of the bell (fig. 21), and cut the shape out of a white card. Make an enclosed shape (see page 30, fig. 2) and two enclosed bands across the bell (fig. 21). Fill the shapes as shown. If gold or silver is desired, use spray paint. Fill in with crimped shapes and double pinched coils between the bands, using a color that contrasts with the color of the bell.

Make a lattice, and cut it to fit. For the flower, cut three petals (see fig. 9), and make flowers as described on page 33, adding glitter and wire edges. Attach the petals to a conical coil.

To make a greeting card, cut a 10″ x 7″ piece of heavy paper, and fold it in half. Or you can mount the bell on a 5″ x 7″ piece of card. Assemble. Glue on the lattice piece, and glue the bell in place, overlapping the lattice slightly. Add a band, enclosing the remaining lattice edge, and a few scrolls around the lattice. Glue on a pinched coil for the clapper, then glue the flower in position. Add a narrow ribbon bow, gluing the ends to hold them.

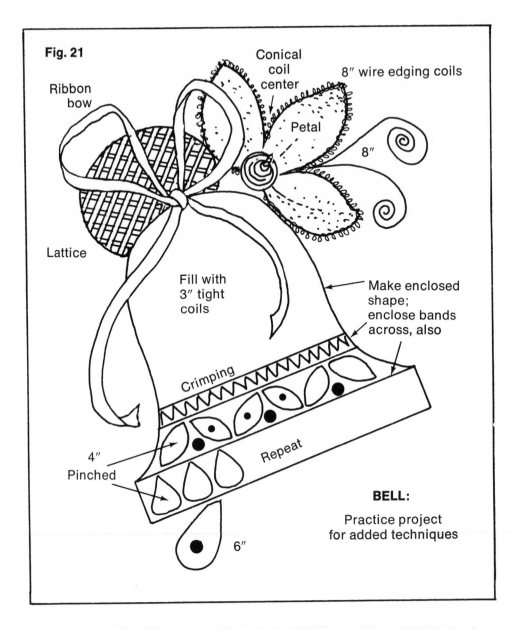

Fig. 21

Ribbon bow

Conical coil center

8″ wire edging coils

Petal

8″

Lattice

Fill with 3″ tight coils

Make enclosed shape; enclose bands across, also

Crimping

4″ Pinched

Repeat

BELL:

Practice project for added techniques

6″

In the center of each double pinched shape, glue a flat-backed jewel, and use a larger jewel on the clapper. Add any other trims you like.

Hand deliver this card. If desired, the card can be placed in a shallow box with a transparent top (from notes or stationery). Plan your card size to fit the box available.

MOUNTINGS, PATTERNS, AND OTHER NOTES

Backings

Most quilled designs are attached directly to a background, put in a frame with some depth, and hung on a wall. However, other uses and suggestions are given throughout this book.

For backing, corrugated cardboard may be used since quilling can be pinned in position when gluing units in place. Art stores and some craft suppliers carry a foam core board that is ³⁄₁₆″ thick (designed as a substitute for corrugated cardboard). This is excellent for backing because it warps less and quilled units can be pinned into place easily.

The backing can be covered with all sorts of materials. You can use gift wraps, plain or textured, and glue them to the backing with rubber cement. Velvet, felt, brocade, and other fabric backgrounds enhance your design and add elegance, but be careful that they don't overpower delicate quilling. Glue these on with Sobo.

Quilling can also be glued onto a wooden cutting board or other wooden plaques (fig. 1). Finish the surface of the wood first.

Fig. 1

Stilts And Layering

Certain quilled pieces look more exciting if they are slightly raised from the backing. Make several tight coils for stilts or pegs. Glue the stilts on the back of the completed piece, then glue the stilts to the backing (fig. 2).

Quilling designs can be built up with two or three layers. Add coils and scrolls over a design like the cross (page 20), giving it extra dimension (fig. 3). Attach the finished piece to the background with stilts, and place it in a deep shadow-box frame.

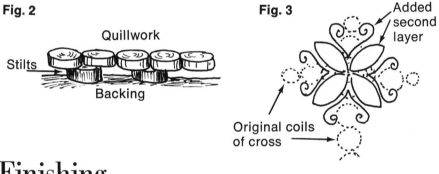

Fig. 2

Quillwork

Stilts

Backing

Fig. 3

Added second layer

Original coils of cross

Finishing

Quilling that is not covered with glass may be sprayed with a clear plastic finish (available from art-supply or craft stores). There are several brands, such as Krylon, Blair, and Eagle; follow the directions on the can. Brush-on coating, such as Activa Glaze or other decoupage finishes, gives a hard, clear covering. Clear nail polish will give the same effect; translucent polish imparts a sheen to the curled paper (see the jewelry on page 74).

Framing

The only real expense in quilling is the framing, as a certain depth (at least $\frac{3}{16}''$) is needed below the glass. Frames can vary considerably in price. Some plastic ones often look almost as elegant as the more expensive wood or metal frames. Since most quilling is small, some photograph frames available in variety stores may be deep enough. Small frames often have thick cardboard in back; this can be removed to allow room for your quilling. Mount the quilling on a lightweight card and insert it in the frame. Check garage and rummage sales for shadow boxes or frames having a little depth. Wooden servers with cutouts for tiles can be used to hold quilling.

A small framed or mounted design can be displayed on a little table easel (fig. 4).

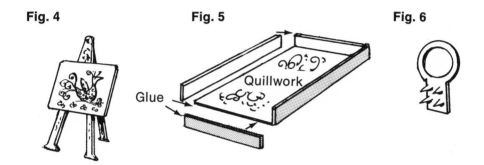

Fig. 4   **Fig. 5**   **Fig. 6**

Glue   Quillwork

Shadow Boxes

You can make a shadow box if you have a few hand tools. Wooden strips 1″ x 3″ x 8′ are available in lumberyards. If you don't have access to a lumber store, you can use a wooden yard-stick as a substitute. Cut the lengths needed to edge the cardboard backing of quilling. (If the cardboard has warped, glue on another piece with corrugations in the other direction.) Sand, then paint the wooden strips. Add glue to the edges and corners (fig. 5), and glue them to the board. Glue a hanger (fig. 6) onto the back of the card.

To make a sturdier shadow box, use a wooden back cut to size. Glue the card with your quilling onto the wooden backing; glue and nail wooden strips around the sides. To make the shadow box more complete, have a piece of glass cut to fit. Glue it on the front, and cover the sharp edges with cloth tape.

Patterns

Most patterns are given actual size. Lay tracing paper over the design and trace, then place the tracing beneath the waxed paper. Sometimes, when a pattern repeats, only one section is given. Trace this section, turn the paper, trace on another segment, and repeat to complete the pattern (fig. 7).

Some patterns will need enlarging. On a piece of tracing paper, draw squares ¼″ apart. Lay the paper over the design in the book. On a larger piece of paper, draw squares 1″ apart. Using the small squares as a guide, draw an outline on the larger squares (fig. 8). Make the lines correspond, square for square, to the lines in the small drawing.

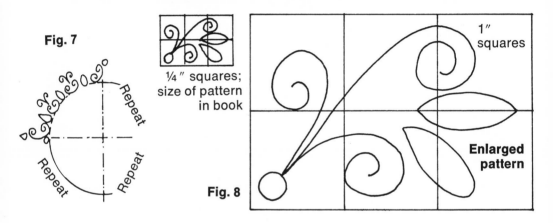

Fig. 7

¼″ squares; size of pattern in book

1″ squares

Enlarged pattern

Fig. 8

Quilling For Children

Some projects in this book can be made by children as well as adults. When children curl and glue paper, keep plenty of damp cloths ready for sticky hands. Draw lines on construction paper ⅜″ or ¼″ apart. Let the children cut, with scissors, the strips for quilling. Hatpins may be too sharp for very young children, but they can use a round toothpick or a fine-gauge knitting needle to roll coils. "T" pins, used for macramé, can be used for pinning coils onto the corrugated board. Let the children use their own ideas—don't expect them to stick exactly to the pattern.

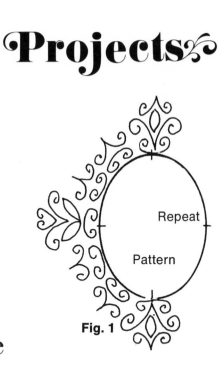

Fig. 1

Projects

Quill An Oval Frame

A favorite print or photograph becomes a treasure when it is surrounded by a quilled frame. Try to keep a proper scale: the quilling shouldn't overwhelm the center unit, colors should harmonize or enhance.

Materials needed: ⅛″ quilling strips; picture or medallion; backing, and frame to fit.

Choose a photograph or a picture from a greeting card, calendar, brochure, or old print. Cut it into a round or oval shape.

The quilled frame shown surrounds a ceramic oval medallion 1½″ high (available from jewelry suppliers; see page 125). Trace the pattern (fig. 1), then trace the other half to make a complete pattern. Place the pattern under the waxed paper. Trace an oval outline to use as a guide for selecting and cutting a picture. Cut picture oval shape or use medallion.

First, quill the units shown in fig. 2, then fill curves between with scrolls. Add pearls or jewels if desired. Remove the frame from the waxed paper, and glue it to the picture or medallion. Glue the unit onto a dark background, and put it into a frame with glass. Or mount the unit on a plaque.

Fig. 2

Side

Top

Fig. 3

Condensed

Stretched

Most repeat quilling patterns are easy to adapt to any size. Quill the top, bottom, and each side unit (fig. 2), add or subtract enough repeat scrolls between to complete the frame. Most scrolls can be stretched or condensed as needed (fig. 3). If they are consistent, they look attractive either way. Other patterns for various size and shape frames are shown in fig. 4.

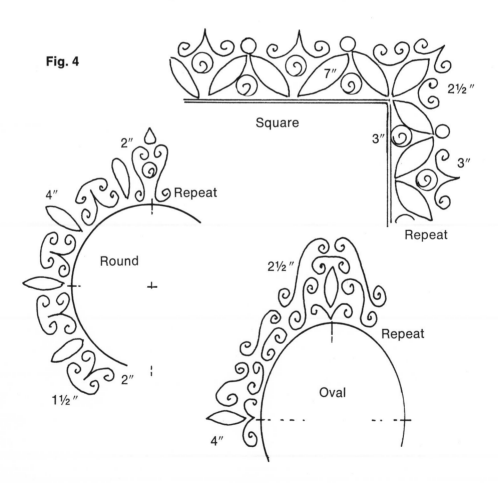

Fig. 4

7″

2½″

Square

3″

3″

Repeat

2″

4″

Repeat

Round

1½″

2″

2½″

Repeat

Oval

4″

Cock And Hen (Antique-Inspired)

A large antique wall sconce was the original inspiration for my involvement in the art of quilling. Part of the New York Metropolitan Museum of Art's collection, this sconce (dating from around 1730) has many elements: a vase with mica-covered flowers, coral, shells, wire, crimping, and other things hard to identify. I made a number of sketches of the various components and chose the cock and hen motif for my first quilling.

Materials needed: ³⁄₁₆″ tan or yellow quilling papers; gold spray; a piece of lightweight card; translucent glitter; gold beading wire; a few seashells (if you have them); a 9″ x 11″ piece of black felt, velvet, or other fabric; a deep 9″ x 11″ frame.

Trace the pattern (fig. 1). Trace two bird bodies on lightweight card, and cut them out. Cut a 10″ strip of quilling paper. Glue the strip around one shape, starting at the beak, to make an enclosed shape. Trim the end at the beak, and glue to make a pointed beak. Repeat for the other bird, making sure it faces in the reverse direction. Make three pinched shapes for each wing, and open coil for the eye of each bird. Glue in position. Fill in the rest of the body with tight coils. Glue on the tail curls, wattles, and feet. For the cock, make a comb (see pattern); for the hen, fold a strip (fig. 2) like crimping, and glue to the head.

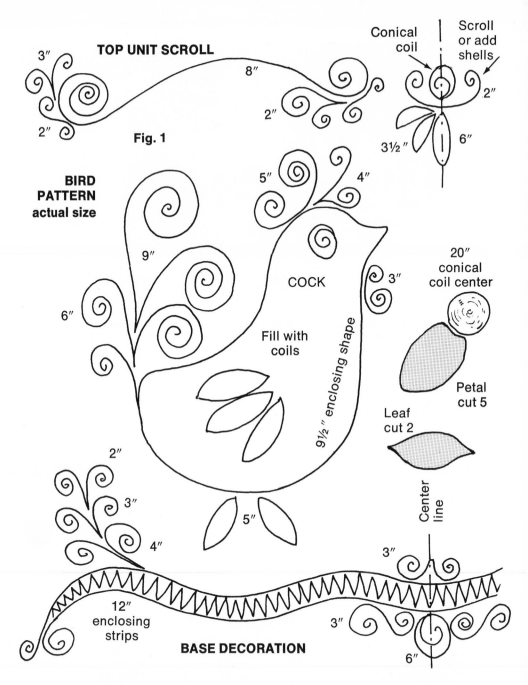

TOP UNIT SCROLL

3″

8″

2″

2″

Fig. 1

Conical coil

Scroll or add shells

2″

3½″

6″

BIRD PATTERN actual size

5″

4″

9″

COCK

3″

6″

Fill with coils

9½″ enclosing shape

20″ conical coil center

Petal cut 5

Leaf cut 2

2″

3″

4″

5″

Center line

3″

12″ enclosing strips

3″

BASE DECORATION

6″

To make the base decoration, trace the half shape shown in the pattern, then fold the paper and trace the other half. Make an enclosed shape for crimping. Scroll the ends of the enclosing strips (fig. 3). Make crimping (page 31), and glue in place. Glue on scrolls as indicated in the pattern.

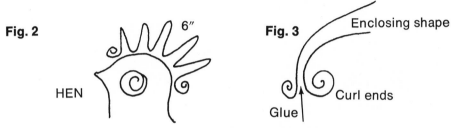

Fig. 2

6"

HEN

Fig. 3

Enclosing shape

Curl ends

Glue

Quill the scroll for the top, making a unit for each side. For the center design, make a low conical coil. Make five pinched coils, and glue them to the top tight coil (see fig. 4). Lightly spray-paint all quilled units gold.

Trace the flower petal and leaf. Cut five petals and two leaves out of lightweight card. Paint the petals a dusty rose color, the leaves a gray-green. When they are dry, apply the glitter. Edge the units with wire coils (see page 32). Make a conical coil from a 12" strip. Glue the petals to the coil using a temporary collar (see page 33).

When all the units are dry, assemble the picture. Glue the black fabric to the backing card that comes with the frame. Position the birds on the background, facing each other, the flower in the center. Make a stem from a wire coil pulled out to 1½" (fig. 5). Place the unit with the crimping at the base, the other units at top (see photograph). When you are satisfied with the arrangement, glue units in place. On either side of the top-center unit (see fig. 4), place a seashell (or a pinched coil). Place a seashell about ¾" long (or a pinched coil) at either side of the base of the flower (see fig. 5).

Place the complete design in its frame.

Fig. 4

Shells

Top center unit

Fig. 5

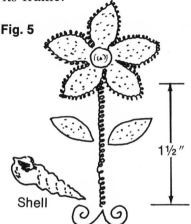

1½"

Shell

Framing With Found Objects

A purchased frame obviously is the best way to display quilling, but with ingenuity, less expensive mountings can be found: household discards such as jar tops, shallow cans, or the protective clear plastic bubbles that cover so many small objects when purchased. How often do you buy a small gadget, remove the card backing and discard the plastic bubble? Other plastics such as clear boxes and bottles may also be used.

Materials: ⅛″ or ³⁄₁₆″ colorful quilling paper; jar tops or plastic bubbles; card, wood, or fabric for backing.

To make the panel shown in fig. 1, find three jar tops of the same size. Spray or paint them black or gold. Draw the inside diameter of the jar top on a piece of colorful card, and

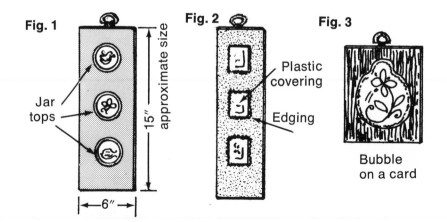

Fig. 1

Jar tops

15″ approximate size

|←— 6″ —→|

Fig. 2

Plastic covering

Edging

Fig. 3

Bubble on a card

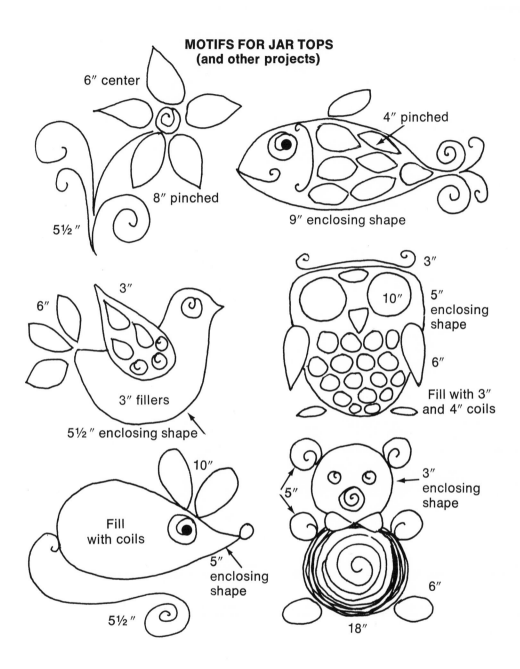

MOTIFS FOR JAR TOPS
(and other projects)

6″ center

4″ pinched

8″ pinched

5½″

9″ enclosing shape

3″

6″

3″ fillers

5½″ enclosing shape

3″

5″ enclosing shape

6″

Fill with 3″ and 4″ coils

10″

Fill with coils

5″ enclosing shape

5½″

10″

5″

3″ enclosing shape

6″

18″

cut out the shape. Select three of the simple designs shown above. Quill units to fit the card and glue on; glue into jar tops. Cut a heavy card or wood backing to the proper size (fig. 1), and glue on the three jar tops. Attach a decorative hanger to the top.

SMALL MOTIFS FOR BUBBLES (and other projects)

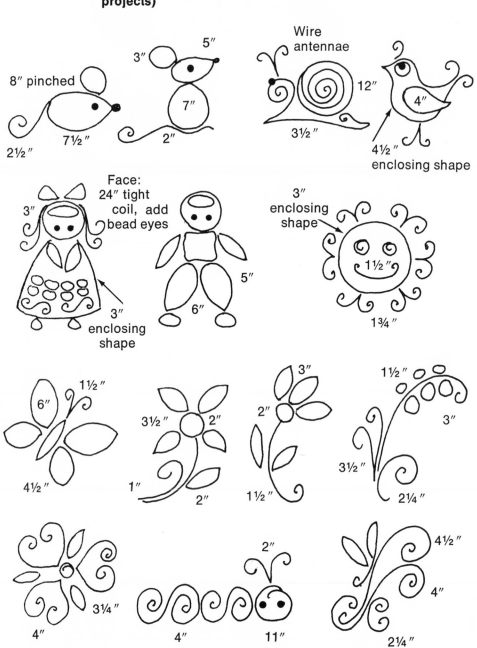

8″ pinched

3″   5″

Wire antennae

2½″   7½″

7″   2″

12″

3½″

4″

4½″
enclosing shape

3″
Face:
24″ tight
coil, add
bead eyes

3″
enclosing
shape

5″

1½″

6″   2″

1¾″

3″
enclosing
shape

1½″

6″   1½″

3½″   2″

3″

1½″

3″

1″   2″

1½″

3½″

2¼″

3¼″

4″

2″

4″   11″

4½″

4″

2¼″

If a protective covering is desired, smooth plastic food wrap around and to back of each unit before gluing unit onto the background.

To make fig. 2, find three similar bubbles. The ones shown came from a dime store's hardware department. Cut colored cards to fit the back of each bubble. Select a motif from the opposite page and make quilling to fit. Glue the designs to the card backing, and then glue a bubble over each. Cut a backing of heavy card or wood, large enough to display the units, and glue the quilling into position. Glue a cord or decorative paper edging around each plastic shape to hide any unsightly edges.

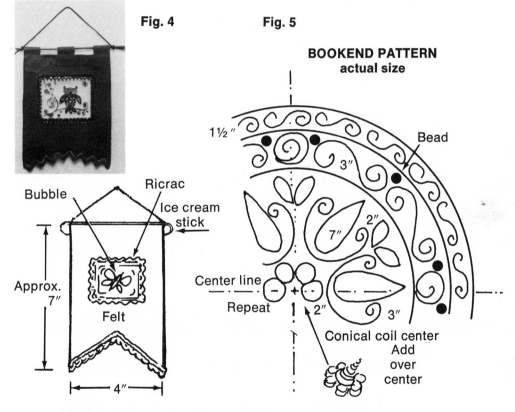

Fig. 4

Fig. 5

BOOKEND PATTERN
actual size

1½"

3"

Bead

Bubble

Ricrac

Ice cream stick

Approx. 7"

Felt

7"

2"

Center line

Repeat

2"

3"

Conical coil center
Add over center

4"

Single units can be effective also (fig. 3), using larger tops or bubbles. Or try mounting a small bubble on felt (fig. 4).

In the same manner, make a bookend using a large top such as the 6″ plastic cover of an ice cream container. Spray the cover gold. The design in fig. 5 was inspired by a filigree brooch.

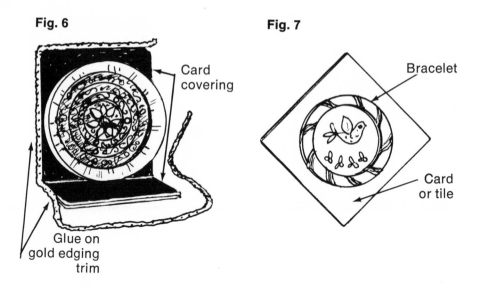

Fig. 6

Card covering

Glue on gold edging trim

Fig. 7

Bracelet

Card or tile

Make quilling and spray it gold. Cut a blue circle to fit inside the cover, and glue it in. Glue in the quilled unit and add gold beads.

Trace around the upright section of a plain metal bookend. Cut two pieces of card this size, and glue to each side of the upright section. Cover the base by cutting a piece of card to fit. Paint card or cover with fabric or paper. Glue the quilled unit (fig. 6) to the covered bookend. Glue gold trim around all the edges.

Any of the small designs in this book can be adapted to this sort of mounting. Other objects that could frame quilling include a bracelet (fig. 7), a coaster, casters, or shallow cans (fig. 8)—how about a quilled fish in a sardine can!

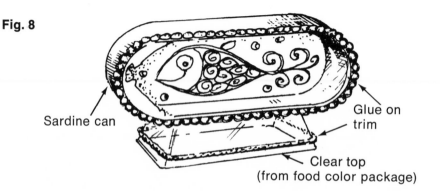

Fig. 8

Sardine can

Glue on trim

Clear top (from food color package)

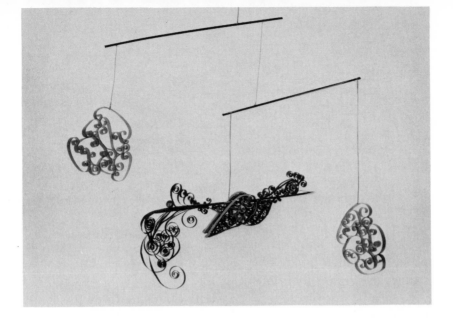

Bird Mobile

Quilled mobiles respond to the slightest movement of air because they are so light weight. Birds are a most appropriate subject. Make several birds and hang them at various levels, or make one bird and add some clouds.

Materials needed: ⅛" white and colored paper strips; 6½" stick (a wooden skewer from an Oriental novelty store, a thin dowel, or a long matchstick); other sticks for hanging; nylon fishline.

A stick in the center of the bird gives rigidity and needed weight. Trim one end to a point for the beak. Quill the bird body (fig. 1), and glue it to the stick. Glue the ends of the tail scrolls

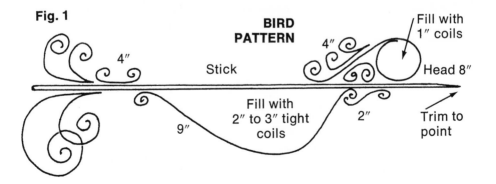

Fig. 1

BIRD PATTERN

Stick

4"

4"

Fill with 1" coils

Head 8"

9"

Fill with 2" to 3" tight coils

2"

Trim to point

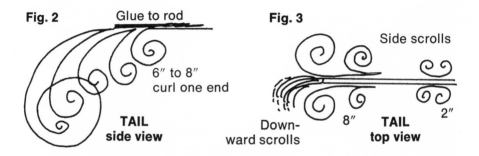

Fig. 2

Glue to rod

6" to 8"
curl one end

TAIL
side view

Fig. 3

Side scrolls

Down-
ward scrolls

8"

TAIL
top view

2"

together, and glue them to the rod (fig. 2). Add side scrolls to the tail for dimension (fig. 3). Curl and twist tail scrolls downward, arranging them attractively.

Glue a 1" strip to the head, and fold it to form the beak (fig. 4). Add two "V" scrolls on top of the head. Trace the wing pattern (fig. 5), quill two and glue them to either side of the body.

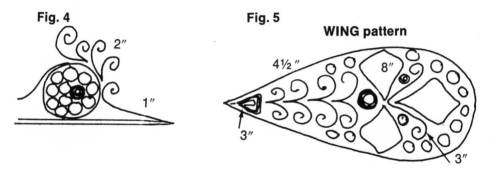

Fig. 4

2"

1"

Fig. 5

WING pattern

4½"

8"

3"

3"

To balance the bird, insert a hatpin between the coils and hold it up to determine the point to attach the hanging line (fig. 6). When the stick rests on a horizontal, tie on the transparent line at that point and suspend the bird.

Make the other elements of the mobile. Clouds, about 2" in diameter, could be any random loose coils and "S" curve

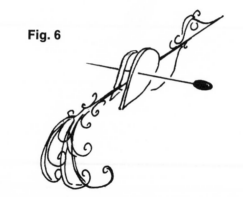

Fig. 6

Fig. 7   **CLOUD**

scrolls (fig. 7 is just a suggestion). Determine the balance of each unit and tie on a line.

Hang the elements from a small embroidery hoop (fig. 8), or use two skewers, sticks, or thin dowels (see photograph). Tie on lines, and slide them back and forth until balance points are found. Add a touch of glue at each balance point, and hang up your mobile.

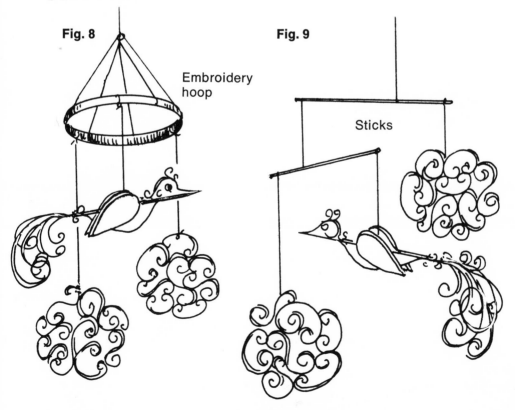

Fig. 8

Embroidery hoop

Fig. 9

Sticks

Bracelet Sculpture

Not all quilling has to be hung up. Why not try making a coffee-table piece with a contemporary, "art deco" feeling?

Materials needed: ⅛″ or ³⁄₁₆″ quilling strips; three inexpensive gold or silver metal bracelets (from the dime store); thin wire coat hanger; lightweight card; piece of ¾″ thick wood about 3″ x 4½″; gold (or silver) spray.

Tools needed: awl; cutting pliers; small hand drill.

Cut three strips of card ³⁄₁₆″ wider than the width of each bracelet and ¼″ longer than the circumference. Curl them around the insides of the bracelets, and glue the cardboard ends together. Do not glue the strip to the bracelet; use it only to maintain a circular shape until it is time to spray-paint the unit. Remove the bracelet while painting.

Draw three circles on paper, tracing the inside of each shape on cardboard. Trace the designs shown (fig. 1), adjust them to fit your circles, and quill the designs.

Using cutting pliers, cut the wire coat hanger (or similar thickness of wire) into three pieces, 5½″, 6½″, and 9″. With the awl, make a hole in the edge of the cardboard next to the bracelet (fig. 2). Push the end of one piece of wire through the hole, until it touches the other side (fig. 3). Add glue to secure it in position. Repeat for the other two circles.

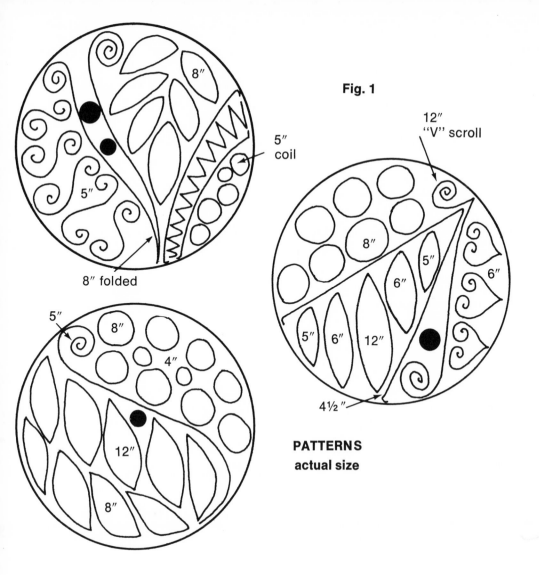

Fig. 1

5″ coil

12″ "V" scroll

8″

8″ folded

5″

PATTERNS
actual size

Glue a quilled unit inside each cardboard circle and over the wire, placing them as near to the center of the depth as possible.

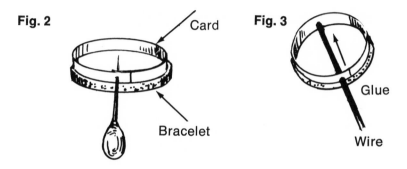

Fig. 2

Card

Bracelet

Fig. 3

Glue

Wire

When the glue is dry, remove the bracelets, and spray quilling, card, and wires with gold paint (or silver if you are using silver bracelets). When the paint is dry, spray the units with a plastic finish. Add glue, and slide the bracelets back into position.

For the base, use natural wood, waxed, or paint the base black.

To position the units, mark a center point on the base and a point 1" on either side. With a small hand drill, make a hole at these points. Add glue to the holes, set the end of each wire into a hole, placing the longest unit in the center (fig. 4). Angle the circles so each is facing a different direction. When the glue is dry, glue a piece of felt to the bottom of base to complete. Add gold beads to quilling if desired.

Fig. 4

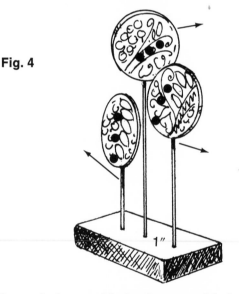

MOBILE: These circles could also be assembled to form a mobile. Omit the wire, quill the units, paint and place them in the bracelets, and tie a cord to the edge of each bracelet. Hang them from a stick or from an embroidery hoop (see page 53).

If you are hanging the mobile near a window, you can add color by cutting a piece of colored cellophane slightly larger than each circle, placing it over the piece, then sliding the bracelet over, and gluing it in place. Trim edges even.

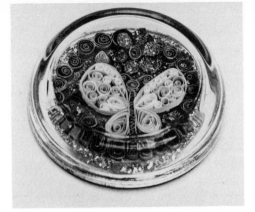

Nostalgic Paperweight

This bit of quilling makes a welcome gift. Select a modern quilled motif (such as the ones shown on page 47), or make it with an antique look.

As the glass used for covering will vary greatly in size, the instructions cannot be too specific. You will have to adjust the design to size, adding or eliminating motifs.

First, select the paperweight cover: a plain glass caster (sold to put under furniture feet) or a coaster about 3″ to 3½″ in diameter. Inverted, this forms the covering for the quilling. A glass lid, old clock face, or any small dome or glass circle that might be found at secondhand sales can be used.

Materials needed: Cover; ⅛″ quilling paper in various colors; beads; glitter; wire; cardboard.

Measure the inside diameter of the glass shape, and cut a cardboard circle to size. Trace around the outside of the glass, and cut another cardboard circle for the base. Set these aside. For the background of the quilling, cover the smaller circle with black or brown paper (or paint). On tissue paper, trace the circle and plan the size for your quilling. The butterfly (fig. 1)

Fig. 1

Quilled butterfly

Flower: quill or make with glitter

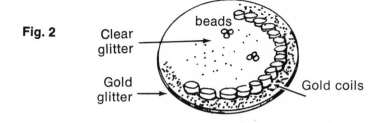

Fig. 2

Clear glitter

beads

Gold glitter

Gold coils

may be too large for some glass pieces; reduce and simplify if necessary. Quill it of various colors. If there is room, add a flower. Cut petals; paint, and assemble them on yellow center tight coil. Add glitter and edging (see page 32) or quill a flower.

About ⅛″ from the edge of the card, make a circle of tight coils, gluing them to each other but not to the backing. Remove, and spray this border gold. When it is dry, glue it in place.

Place the other units in position. Add dabs of glue and gold glitter to spots around the quilled units (fig. 2). Glue on tiny seed beads or other decorations. Add gold glitter to the cardboard outside the border of coils.

When the glue is dry, shake off all extra sprinkles. Glue in the butterfly, attaching its body to the background. Let the wings rest on the edging coils. This raises the wings off the surface for dimension—but check to make sure there is room in your dome. Glue the flower at a slightly raised angle also, if possible (fig. 3).

When all units are dry, spread household cement along edge of the cardboard and glue the glass over the quilling. Glue the larger cardboard circle to the base. Cut a felt circle the same size and glue it onto the base.

Fig. 3

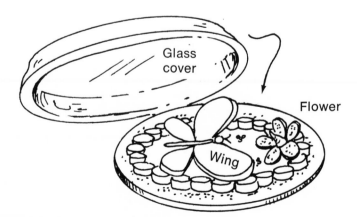

Glass cover

Flower

Wing

Animals

Some types of animals' fur suggests a quilled texture. Animals are fun to do. If a youngster makes an animal, mount it on paper or a card and tack it on a bulletin board. When the animal is quilled by an adult, mount it on a fabric background. Place it in a deep frame with glass if desired. These animals make an attractive decoration for a small child's room.

  Materials needed: For a child's project, cut quilling paper ½″ wide. Adults could use ⅜″ wide strips and fabric backgrounds. Also needed: colored posterboard; foam core board (or corrugated board) for mounting; fabric tape for edges.

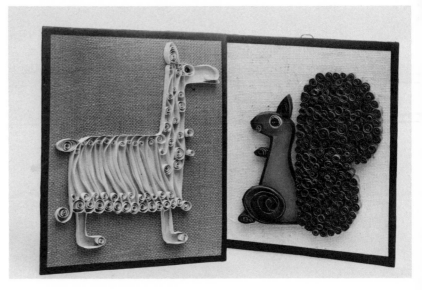

General instructions: Enlarge the pattern of the animal you wish to make. For backing the quilled coils of the body, use a heavy paper or colored cardboard such as posterboard. Select a color that will show up the coils.

Cut the body outline shape out of the card. Make a boxful of coils in varying diameters, using strips 3″ to 6″ long. Glue the coils around and overlapping the edges of the cardboard shape to outline the area (fig. 1). When the outline row is dry, fill the inside, gluing coils to each other and to the backing.

For body areas not covered with quilling, make enclosed shapes (see page 30), gluing the strips (fig. 2) to the edge of card and to the coils (not necessary on children's version). For an eye, make an open white coil, and glue a tight black coil inside.

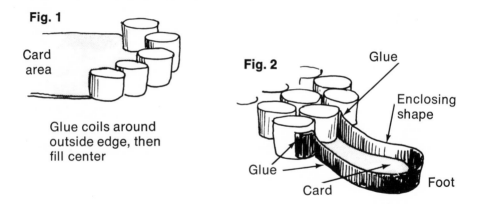

Fig. 1

Card area

Glue coils around outside edge, then fill center

Fig. 2

Glue

Enclosing shape

Glue

Card

Foot

POODLE: Cut the body outline out of a white card, then glue black paper over center body, feet and head (areas without coils). Fill the remaining areas with black coils.

For the ear, cut a 5″ long black strip, place it over the drawing of the shape, and pin. Fill it with black coils. Insert into

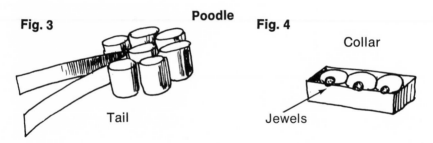

Fig. 3

Poodle

Tail

Fig. 4

Collar

Jewels

PATTERNS: Draw ¼″ squares; enlarge to 1″ squares

position on the head and glue. The nose is a 12″ tight coil. For the tail, fold a 5″ black strip in half and glue medium-size coils (fig. 3) to the end. Cut short strips of black and glue to the edge of the card, making enclosed-shape edges for the body, feet and head (see fig. 2).

For the collar, cut a 4″ enclosing strip of bright-colored paper. Fold and glue in position. Make three coils of another bright color; glue them in. Glue on three jewels (fig. 4).

SHEEP: Cut the shape from a black card, glue on white coils. For the edge of the face, cut two black strips 2″ long. Shape them as shown to form a mouth (fig. 5). Add glue to the edges and attach the face to the edge of the cardboard. For the ear, cut the shape out of a black card, and glue it into position on top of the coils. For the tail, coil a 12″ white strip, pinch one end, shape it and glue it in place. Glue black edgings to the feet and legs (see fig. 2).

Fig. 5   **Sheep**

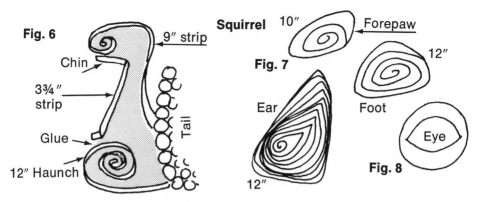

SQUIRREL: Use a yellow background for the tail, orange for the body. Fill the tail with quilled orange and brown coils. Use brown to make the body outline. Wind a 12″ strip around a pencil, then allow the strip to uncurl. Starting at the tail, glue the strip along the edge of the card at the base and up and around to form the haunch (fig. 6). For body front cut a 3¾″ strip, and glue it to the edge of the card from the top of the haunch to the front of the chin. Cut a 9″ piece, curl one end, and glue the straight end to the back at the tail, up and around. The curl makes the mouth; glue it to the end of the last strip.

Quill the ear, forepaw, and foot in the sizes shown (fig. 7). Glue them to body outline strips. For the eye, make a loose coil from a 10″ white strip, then make a 4″ pinched black coil for the center (fig. 8).

PATTERNS: Draw ¼″ squares; enlarge to 1″ squares

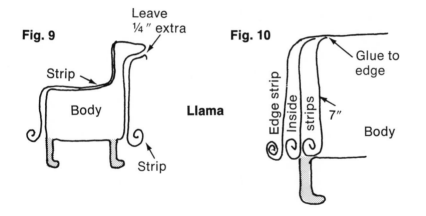

Fig. 9

Leave ¼″ extra

Strip

Body

Llama

Fig. 10

Glue to edge

Edge strip

Inside strips

7″

Body

Strip

LLAMA: Cut the body out of a lavender or blue card, and glue on dark-gray feet. Make body of white strips. Curl ends and glue strips along the edges as shown (fig. 9). For the body, curl and glue in 7″ strips (fig. 10). Keep the space between each strip open, and fill it in with 6″ strips coiled in "S" curves, with a larger scroll at the bottom (fig. 11). Glue them into position. Fill the neck as shown (fig. 12).

For the top of the head and the mouth, curl one end of a strip as shown (fig. 13), and glue. For the eye, make an open circle of a 4″ white strip; add a tight black coil in the center. Glue it in place. For the ear, coil a 12″ strip, pinch, and shape (fig. 14).

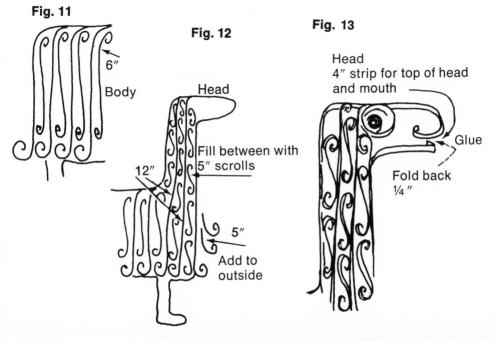

Fig. 11

6″

Body

Fig. 12

Head

Fill between with 5″ scrolls

12″

5″

Add to outside

Fig. 13

Head
4″ strip for top of head and mouth

Glue

Fold back ¼″

For the tail, coil a 9″ strip, pinch one end, and glue it on. For the feet, coil one end of a 5″ strip to make the toes (fig. 15). Glue strips along the edges to enclose the foot shape.

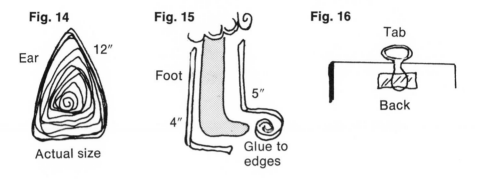

Fig. 14

Ear   12″

Actual size

Fig. 15

Foot

5″

4″

Glue to edges

Fig. 16

Tab

Back

TO MOUNT ANIMALS: Cut a piece of corrugated or foam core board 10″ x 11¾″. Glue on colored paper, fabric, felt, or burlap. Stick-on burlap textures are good. Select a bright color that shows up the animal. Finish the board by sticking fabric tape along the edges. Glue a flat picture hanger onto the back, or tape on a soda-can pull tab (fig. 16). Glue the quilled unit into position.

Three animals could be mounted together on a long board for a mural. Fill in between them with some quilled flowers (fig. 17).

Let children try making other animals. These four should give them ideas. Creatures like the lion, ostrich, fish, or fox would adapt to quilling. Use pictures from coloring books for outlines to quill a menagerie.

Fig. 17

Paper Mosaic Mirror Frame

Some colonial quillers made paper mosaics by completely covering a surface with tight coils of various colors. On a frame for a looking glass from the Shelbourne Museum, (page 12), mosaics surround ovals of old colored engravings. Natural elements and wax figures with real hair had been added to the composition.

To make a mirror frame of paper mosaics is not difficult; it just takes a great deal of time and patience.

Materials needed: ³/₁₆″ or ¼″ quilling strips of assorted colors; round mirror about 5″ diameter. Novelty shops carry mirrors with a cardboard frame that can be removed, or you can buy an inexpensive hand mirror in a plastic frame. Heat the plastic in hot water and force the mirror out.

Other materials: 12″ square of foam core (or corrugated) board; lightweight card; roll of gold cord (sold for gift wrap); tubettini; four small prints or engravings. To frame the board, buy a 12″ square frame or use four painted 12″ rulers and one dozen gold upholstery tacks.

For the background, paint the 12″ square, or select a dark-colored or black paper. As the quilling will be of gold and other bright colors, make the background a fairly deep tone. In the example shown, deep purple paper was glued to the backing board.

If the mirror has its own casing (those with cardboard frames usually do), cut a circular hole in the center of the card so the mirror can be glued from behind when the quilling is finished. If the mirror has been removed from a plastic frame, trace around the mirror, centering it on the board. The mirror will be glued onto the board after the quilling is completed.

On tracing paper, draw four 2½" circles, and place them over pictures, selecting four prints. Use old engravings, old greeting cards, photographs, calendar prints—whatever seems appropriate and goes well together. Cut the four circular pictures.

On the background, lightly mark guidelines from each corner to help in the placement of the pictures (fig. 1). The inner edge of each circle should be at least ¾" away from the mirror edge. Draw on the areas to place the pictures.

Make an enclosed shape around the mirror area. Draw a circle on lightweight card the diameter of the mirror. Draw another circle ⅜" larger. Cut out the inside and the outside edge, forming a ⅜" ring. Glue paper strips to each edge, making an enclosed shape. Section the ring into four quarters. Place a pinched coil at each quarter point (fig. 2), and one coil between each. Alternate "S" coils with crimping, gluing them between the pinched coils. For the outside of the enclosed shape, curl one end of a 2" strip. Glue it to the outside. Repeat, and continue around (fig. 3), gluing the ends to the flat end of the last strip.

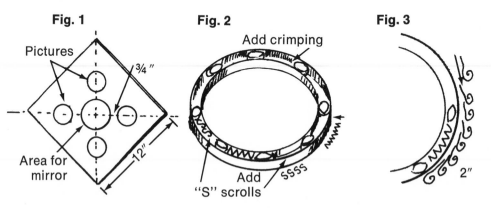

Fig. 1

Pictures

¾"

Area for mirror

12"

Fig. 2

Add crimping

Add "S" scrolls

SSSS

Fig. 3

2"

For the shape around each print, place a 2½" circle under the waxed paper. Cut a strip to fit the circumference, curl around it, and glue to make an edging for each picture (fig. 4). Make a

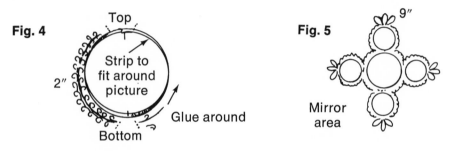

Fig. 4

Top

Strip to fit around picture

2"

Glue around

Bottom

Fig. 5

9"

Mirror area

quilled shape of 2" pieces, and glue it to circle edge, leaving the top and bottom open (fig. 4). Repeat for the other pictures, but do not glue edgings to the pictures.

Place the units on the board to determine the fit. The frames of the pictures should butt against the frame of the mirror. Remove some pieces if necessary. Glue the five frames together as a unit (but don't glue them to the backing). Add three 9" double pinched coils to the outside of each picture frame (fig. 5).

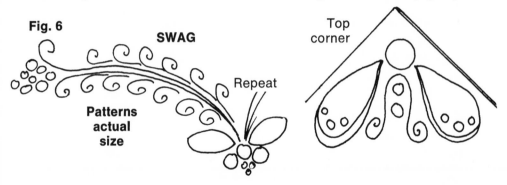

Fig. 6

SWAG

Repeat

Patterns actual size

Top corner

Make the shapes shown (fig. 6). Spray-paint all quilled units gold. When the paint is dry, glue the pictures and frames onto the backing. Glue gold cord around the edges of the mirror and pictures, and onto the edge of the enclosing shape (fig. 7). Glue other gold shapes in position at the top and bottom. Glue gold cord arcs around unoccupied parts of board (fig. 8).

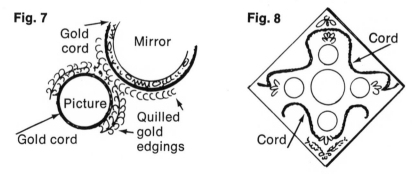

Fig. 7

Gold cord

Mirror

Picture

Gold cord

Quilled gold edgings

Fig. 8

Cord

Cord

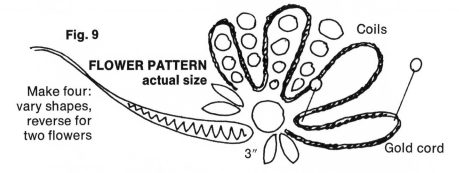

Fig. 9

FLOWER PATTERN
actual size

Make four:
vary shapes,
reverse for
two flowers

Coils

3"

Gold cord

All the remaining space will be filled in with quilled coils in colors (and in gold) for the mosaic effect. Make four flower units (fig. 9), varying each in shape and color. Make a tight center coil, and surround it with gold cord. Pin the gold cord to make a petal shape. Fill it with coils made of 3" to 5" strips. For contrast, use one color between the cords and another color in the spaces. Glue the flowers into position (fig. 10). Make about six small floral units of pinched coils (fig. 11), glue in vacant spots.

Make many colored coils. Glue a section of one color on one side of the gold cord, another color in other sections. Make the coils any size, since they will all fit somewhere. Add more gold cord if you like. Glue in coils as you go along, filling and fitting and grouping colors.

Making tiny coils may become tedious. A similar effect (when combined with quilling) can be achieved by using tubettini (a kind of pasta you'll find in the supermarket). Place a handful in a shallow jar top and spray gold while spraying the other units, or roll tubettini in a puddle of gold around sprayed pieces. Keep turning them as they dry so they won't stick. Glue them to each other and to the backing, holding them with pins through the center. Glue clusters of tubettini into the design wherever small gold accents are needed (fig. 12).

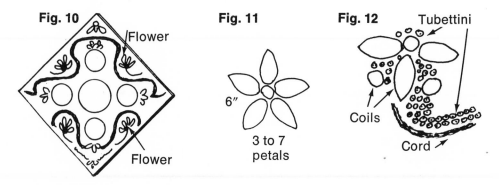

Fig. 10

Flower

Flower

Fig. 11

6"

3 to 7
petals

Fig. 12

Tubettini

Coils

Cord

The mirror is complete when you are satisfied with the effect. Fill the background as loosely or tightly as you like. A true mosaic is tightly filled.

Spray the unit with clear plastic. Glue the mirror into position. To hide the edge of the mirror, cut a $\frac{3}{16}''$ wide strip of card long enough to fit the circumference of the mirror. Paint the strip gold, and glue it inside the quilled circle.

To make an inexpensive edge or frame, use four school rulers (these usually have four holes in them for placing in notebooks). Glue colored tissue or crepe paper over the printed side of the ruler. When the glue is dry, paint both sides of the ruler black or a color that will match the background.

To attach the rulers to the board, add glue to one top edge of the board. Add glue to the tips and under the heads of three tacks. Push the tacks through the holes in one ruler and into the edge of the board, pressing the ruler against the board. Hold with weights pushed against the sides or with large rubber bands. When dry, repeat on other top edge adding glue at ends where rulers meet (fig. 13). Repeat on bottom edges using four tacks on each side.

For a hanging cord, cut an 8″ piece of gold cord. Tie a knot in each end, add glue under the top of two upholstery tacks, and push a tack through each knot. Add glue and put the two tacks with cord attached into upper holes on each side of the top (fig. 14).

Glue gold cord along the edge of the quilling, against the framing (fig. 14), to hide any irregularities in the joining. When all the glue is dry, hang the mirror.

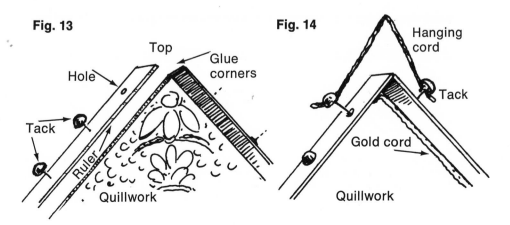

Fig. 13

Top

Hole

Glue corners

Tack

Ruler

Quillwork

Fig. 14

Hanging cord

Tack

Gold cord

Quillwork

Sketch of an English tea caddie (about 1800) covered with quillwork.

Box

English ladies of the eighteenth century decorated many kinds of boxes with quilling, especially tea caddies like the one shown. These boxes were completely covered with coils, using contrasting open and tight coils to create a pattern. It is an interesting effect to re-create.

Materials needed to make box shown: ⅛″ quilling strips in brown and tan plus one bright contrasting color; a wooden box about 5″ x 5″ x 4½″, or any appropriate size; edging cord (or wooden strips for edges); lightweight card; gold paint and brush; brown stain or paint; a medallion (if the box is large enough); decorative picture hanger (used as a handle).

If the box is shallow, keep the details on top, using a simple fill-in design on the sides. If the box is tall enough, plan a motif for the front, such as the one shown. The oval used was a ceramic medallion (from a jewelry supply store; see page 125), but any picture or print could be used.

Stain or paint the box dark brown. For the edges, select a sturdy gold cord, the type sold in craft shops for boutiquing. The cord used here was ⅛″ x ³⁄₁₆″, glued on its edge. Or glue on wooden edges (long matchsticks, ⅛″ square balsa strips, or narrow molding). Stain or paint the wood first. All the sides to be covered with quilling should be completely edged (fig. 1), including the edges where the lip meets the box.

On paper, draw each area (inside the edging) to be filled

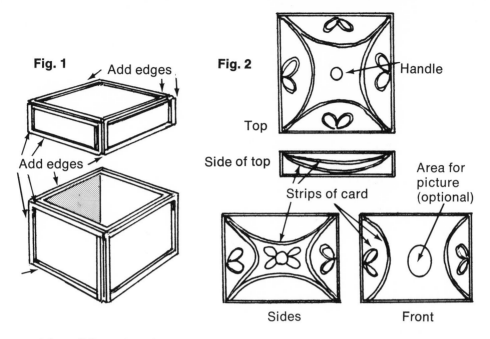

Fig. 1

Add edges

Add edges

Fig. 2

Handle

Top

Side of top

Strips of card

Area for picture (optional)

Sides   Front

with quilling. Starting at each corner, draw curved lines (fig. 2). Within these areas, plan other details, such as the medallion, and in the center of the top, the place to attach a handle. Cut the card into ⅛″ strips. Then cut it into pieces and form the curves (fig. 2). Glue where curves meet.

Cut card for the designs around the medallion (fig. 3) and for design areas for the sides. Shape the card pieces and glue them together, then spray curves and designs gold.

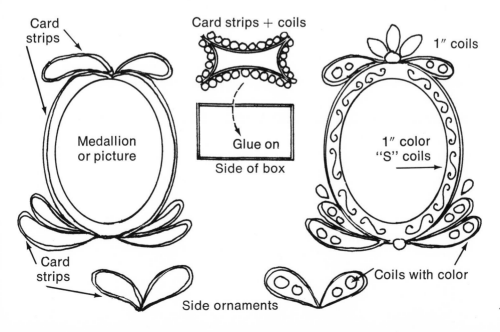

Fig. 3   **Fig. 4**   **Fig. 5**

Card strips

Medallion or picture

Card strips

Card strips + coils

Glue on

Side of box

1″ coils

1″ color "S" coils

Coils with color

Side ornaments

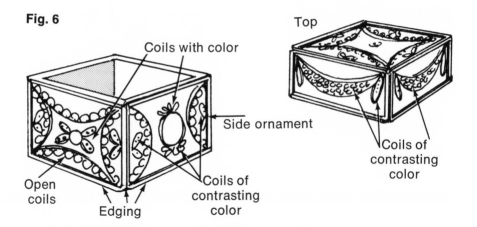

Fig. 6

Coils with color

Top

Side ornament

Open coils

Edging

Coils of contrasting color

Coils of contrasting color

Quill open circles of light tan, curling the paper around a pencil or a large knitting needle so that the centers are open (about ¼″ in diameter). Glue these coils to the curves. Assemble units of curves and glue them to the box (fig. 4), pinning as necessary.

Quill tiny coils of a contrasting color, and glue two in each loop shaped design. Glue colored "S" scrolls around the medallion (fig. 5) and glue the units into position on the box (fig. 6).

Now make quantities of coils of 1″ to 1½″ strips of dark tan or brown, coiling as tightly as possible. Glue on box filling all unoccupied areas.

When the surface is covered, allow the glue to dry thoroughly. To give the effect of gilt-edged paper, carefully paint the top edges of all tan and brown coils with gold paint (see page 16). When the paint is dry, screw the handle to the top of the box, and add feet, nailheads, or felt to finish the bottom.

If you wish, decorate just the top of a box. Many craft shops carry boxes with a recessed area on the top. As these are usually made to hold tiles, the ⅛″ recess is ideal for quilled work. Or an old box may be refinished. If there is no recess, create an edge by gluing on thin strips of wood. Fill the recess with quilling. Many designs in this book are suitable. To make the quilled top more durable, have a piece of glass cut to fit into the recess and glue it over the quillwork inside the wooden edges. Or cut a piece of plastic to fit.

Jewelry And Other Decorations

Delicate, decorative filigree is ideal for jewelry. Quilling can be made durable either by coating it or by embedding it in plastic.

COATED JEWELRY: *Materials needed:* ⅛″ paper; cord, wire, jewels, or beads; coating; jewelry findings for mounting.

    A few suggested shapes and designs are shown (fig. 1). Combine colored paper scrolls with gold or silver cords or trims (from gift wraps or craft supply shops). Such edges enhance the

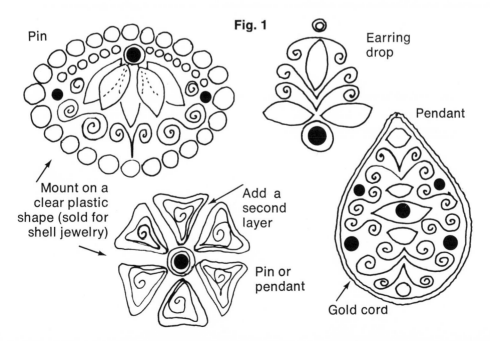

Fig. 1

Pin

Earring drop

Mount on a clear plastic shape (sold for shell jewelry)

Add a second layer

Pin or pendant

Pendant

Gold cord

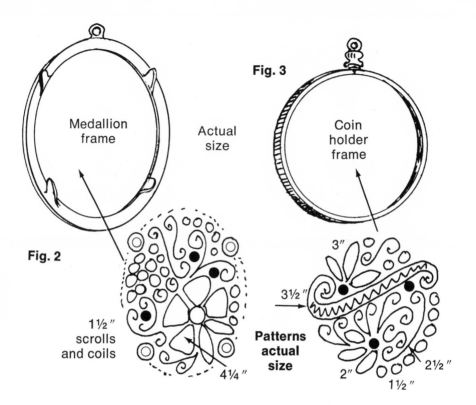

Fig. 3

Medallion frame

Actual size

Coin holder frame

Fig. 2

1½″ scrolls and coils

Patterns actual size

4¼″

3″

3½″

2″

1½″

2½″

design and hold it together. When complete, glue in beads, jewels, or tiny shells.

For other edgings or frames, use circles, such as small curtain rings or bone rings (from knitting departments). Jewelry supply stores (see page 125) and some craft shops carry oval gold frames (fig. 2) for mounting stones or medallions, or round frames for mounting coins (fig. 3). Make quilling to fit the frame selected and glue in.

When the glue is dry, apply a finishing coat, such as Activa Glaze (available in craft supply stores) or a similar product. Follow the instructions on the can. Ordinary nail polish (clear or translucent) can serve the same purpose, making the jewelry quite durable. Cover the paper thoroughly, giving it several coats if necessary.

RESIN CASTING: Attractive jewelry can be made by embedding quilling in plastic. Called resin casting, it comes in kits (such as the "Preserve Forever" kit) with all the materials needed, including small molds. Or you can buy the casting materials in an art

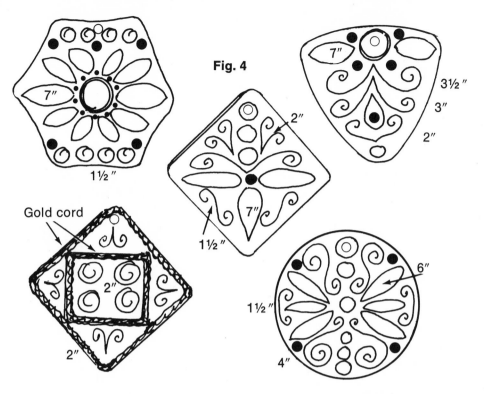

Fig. 4

supply or craft store where you can select the molds and buy the materials separately if you prefer. Some heavy flexible plastics found around the house can be used for molds, such as the top of a coffee or boullion-cube can.

Materials needed: bright or deep-colored ⅛" quilling paper (pale colors tend to get lost); gold cord; beads or jewels; resin casting kit; jewelry findings. Tools needed: hand drill; fine sandpaper, powdered pumice or toothpaste (for finishing).

The quilled design should be fairly tight, since loose scrolls tend to drift somewhat in liquid plastic. Gold cord and beads look good when embedded. Be wary of using gold-sprayed paper because the liquid plastic may dissolve the gold. The designs in fig. 4 are sized to fit standard molds. Any simple design can be adapted.

If you are using a can lid as a mold, fig. 5 suggests two designs. Quill design to fit lid. For birds, cut colored cellophane to fit body areas. Glue on.

Make all the units as complete as possible before mixing the plastic. Make sure the glue is thoroughly dry; let the design dry at least overnight, for there must be *no* moisture present when embedding.

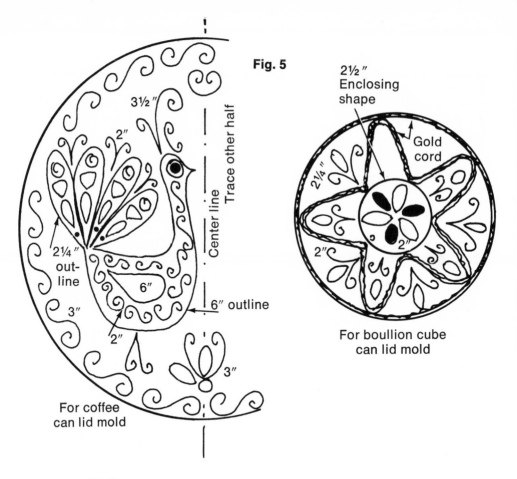

Fig. 5

3½"

2"

2¼"
out-
line

3"

2"

6"

6" outline

Center line

Trace other half

For coffee
can lid mold

2½"
Enclosing
shape

Gold
cord

2¼"

2"

2"

For boullion cube
can lid mold

Follow the instructions in the kit, treating quilling like any embedment (usually a three-layer pouring). Allow the plastic to cure (check instructions). Finish and polish, if necessary, as instructed. If the casting is not perfectly clear, use a little pumice or toothpaste to polish the surface. Drill holes where needed to suspend the castings for pendants or drop earrings.

ASSEMBLING: To assemble coated or cast jewelry, use jewelry findings available in craft stores and from mail-order suppliers (see page 125). Some findings and their uses are shown in fig. 6. Attach where necessary with epoxy glue.

Use jump links to assemble most units. Open a link slightly with narrow-tipped pliers, slip it into the hole in the pendant and over a chain, cord, or thong. Use a link to attach a unit to a drop-earring back (fig. 7). For a linked-type necklace (fig. 8) insert a cast quilled unit between beads.

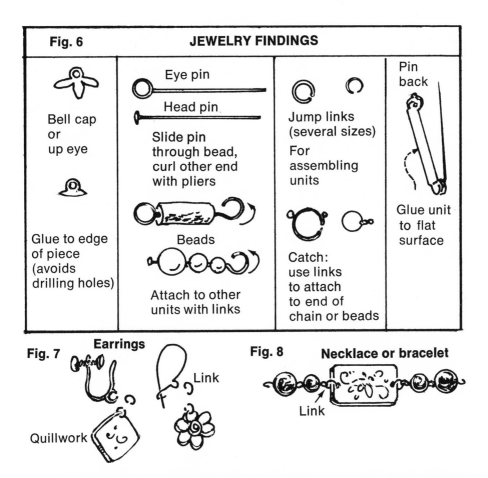

Fig. 6   **JEWELRY FINDINGS**

Bell cap
or
up eye

Glue to edge
of piece
(avoids
drilling holes)

Eye pin

Head pin

Slide pin
through bead,
curl other end
with pliers

Beads

Attach to other
units with links

Jump links
(several sizes)

For
assembling
units

Catch:
use links
to attach
to end of
chain or beads

Pin
back

Glue unit
to flat
surface

Fig. 7   **Earrings**

Link

Quillwork

Fig. 8   **Necklace or bracelet**

Link

To make matching beads, cut pieces of the same paper the quilling strips were cut from. For tubular beads, cut pieces 1″ x 8″ (or whatever size is desired). For oval beads, cut triangles approximately the size shown (fig. 9). Roll the paper on a hatpin about halfway, add glue to rest of strip, and finish rolling (fig. 10).

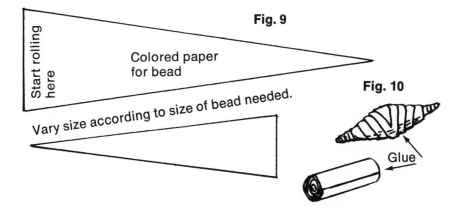

Fig. 9

Start rolling
here

Colored paper
for bead

Vary size according to size of bead needed.

Fig. 10

Glue

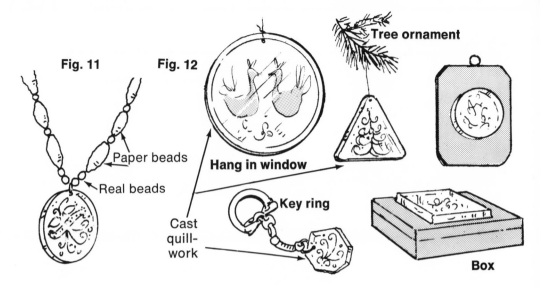

Fig. 11   Fig. 12

Paper beads

Real beads

Cast quill-work

Hang in window

Tree ornament

Key ring

Box

Cover with several coats of finish. String, suspending the quilled pendant in the center (fig. 11).

Many combinations are possible. Look at current jewelry styles to get ideas for shapes and arrangements. Make quilled units into necklaces, pendants, earrings, bracelets, tie clips, pins —almost any jewelry.

OTHER USES FOR PLASTIC CASTINGS: Quilling embedded in plastic is durable enough for many other uses. Units could be used for key rings, box decoration or holiday ornaments (fig. 12). The casting in the coffee can lid can be hung in the window as an ornament or mounted on a bookend or on a board for a wall plaque.

Larger molds are available for casting paperweights, candlesticks, and plaques. Draw a quilling design to fit the mold area, quill and cast. For a paperweight, if the mold is deep enough, make two layers, a small top design, and a quilled base (fig. 13).

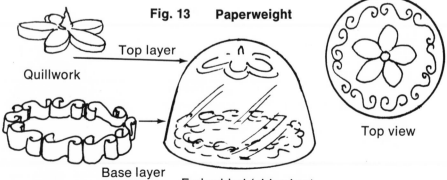

Fig. 13   Paperweight

Quillwork

Top layer

Base layer

Embedded (side view)

Top view

Holidays & Occasions

PARTIES

Paper decorations are appropriate for festive occasions. Quilled trimmings become conversation pieces and add to that "special day" feeling. Decorations could be made for a wall, the table, packages, or favors. Seasonal holidays as well as wedding celebrations, birthdays, showers, and anniversaries create a theme for designs to be quilled. Every celebration has special colors and motifs that can be adapted to quilling.

FAVORS: A handmade party favor will be cherished. Make a simple quilled frame (page 25 or 41) around a picture of the bridal couple or the birthday child. Place it in a simple gold plastic frame. Or quill a flower or a little bird, and mount it on a wood or cardboard plaque that can be hung up (fig. 1). Write the date and occasion on the back. This makes a unique favor that will become a treasured remembrance for each guest.

HATS. For children's parties, buy some plain party hats. Show the children how to curl paper. Have strips of various widths and colors on hand as well as other trimmings, such as feathers, plastic beads, and bright papers, foil, or crepe paper. Let them decorate their own hats (fig. 2). Paper curls can be taped in place with transparent tape.

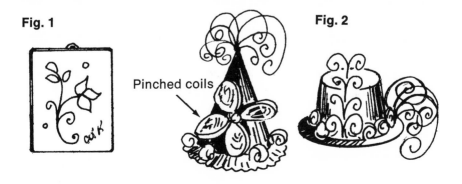

Fig. 1

Pinched coils

Fig. 2

Quilled Wrap-Ups

Wrapping gifts is part of the fun of any occasion. Use your quilling skill. Show you really care. Add quilling to a very special gift. Choose a simple shape (see page 48), or quill the word "LOVE" (see page 88). Using ¼″ strips, adapt the pattern to fit the size of the package.

Wrap the gift in plain colored paper, tissue, or foil. Glue on the quilled shape, add ribbons or bows if needed. If the gift wrap paper is heavy enough, the quilling can be saved when the gift is opened. Carefully cut off the top part of the wrapping and frame or mount it on a board. Another way to re-use quilling is to glue a design onto a clothespin (fig. 7, page 103), and clip it onto the ribbon. Here are a few suggestions for gift wrap decorations.

FLOWERS: Wrap the box in colored tissue. Tape the ribbon around, and tape on ribbon ends (fig. 1). Using two colors, roll two 10″ strips together, making six double pinched coils. Glue them onto the package to make two flowers. Embellish the design with scrolls glued to the top of each flower.

Fig. 1

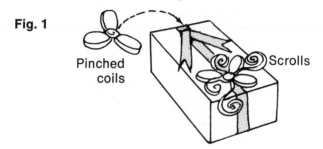

Pinched coils

Scrolls

Fig. 2   Glue

Fig. 3   Glue

BRIDAL SHOWER: Cover the box with blue paper. On a plain piece of paper, draw an umbrella shape that fits the size of the package. Slip the design under the waxed paper. Make an outside strip, curling in both ends. Pin it in place. Cut the next strip about ½″ shorter, and curl both ends. Pin it in place, gluing at the center top and where the coils touch (fig. 2). Continue until the area is filled, holding the center top with a hair clip until the glue dries. Cut the handle and curl it at the bottom. Put the handle through the scrolls and glue it to the top (fig. 3). Make a "V" scroll on top. Add a bow. For a more festive look, glue on dabs of glitter.

BABY SHOWER: Wrap the gift in white or pink and decorate with a fanciful blue stork. Cut two long strips of blue paper, and scroll them for the body as shown (fig. 4). Place the ends of the scrolls together for the head. Glue at the neck and base of the tail. Add a folded scroll for an extra tail piece (fig. 5), three pinched coils for wings, and a yellow inverted "V" for the legs. Make the beak of a yellow folded-heart scroll (fig. 6). Make a tight black coil for the eye. Lift the stork off the board and glue it onto the package; add a bow.

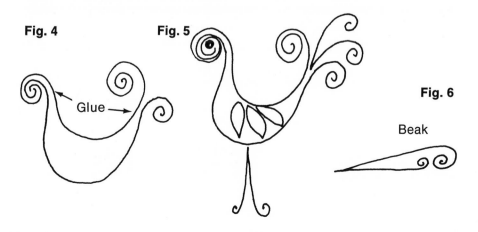

Fig. 4   Fig. 5   Glue →   Fig. 6   Beak

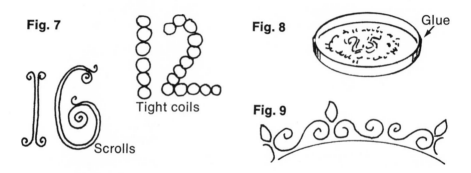

Fig. 7

Fig. 8 Glue

Tight coils

Scrolls

Fig. 9

BIRTHDAY (or anniversary): A quilled frame can enhance a message. Wrap the package in plain color paper. Cut a greeting or motif from a used greeting card or patterned gift wrap paper, making a round or oval shape. Or buy a medallion that states the birthday age or anniversary number. With a little ingenuity (fig. 7), the number could be quilled.

Draw the area to be framed, and place it under the waxed paper. Cut a strip to fit around it, and glue the ends (fig. 8). Quill a simple frame (fig. 9) and glue it to the edging. Glue the motif and frame to the top of the package, and add a bow if desired.

OTHER SUGGESTIONS: Shown below are more ideas (fig. 10), for gift wrap trims for other occasions.

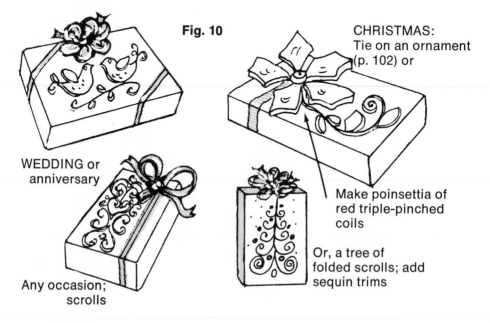

Fig. 10

WEDDING or anniversary

Any occasion; scrolls

CHRISTMAS: Tie on an ornament (p. 102) or

Make poinsettia of red triple-pinched coils

Or, a tree of folded scrolls; add sequin trims

Embellished Wedding Invitation

Embellishing a wedding invitation is a tradition that has recently been revived, and dainty quillwork is especially appropriate. You can arrange and use whatever looks best around the invitation you wish to frame, to give to someone special or to save for your own keepsake. As invitations vary considerably in size and shape, a few motifs and materials will be suggested.

Materials needed: invitation; frame; ⅛″ quilling strips; backing fabric; jewels or pearls; bits of net or ribbon from the bridal bouquet.

Select a frame with sufficient depth. The size should allow at least a 1½″ border around the invitation. Cover the backing card that comes with the frame with paper, velour, or fabric in

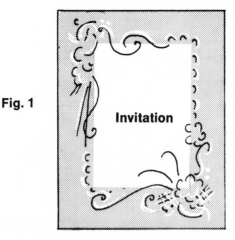

Fig. 1

Invitation

the color of your choice. If the side area (the depth of the frame) shows, cover this with the same color. Use rubber cement to attach the paper, or fabric glue if using fabric. If the invitation is printed on a folded sheet, trim off the blank side and mount the printed side on the background.

Plan your design. Lay the mounted invitation under a piece of tissue paper and trace the outline. Sketch in and plan where to place your quilling (fig. 1). Trace the motifs shown (fig. 2), or make up your own. Scrolls, leaf tendrils, and delicate flowers

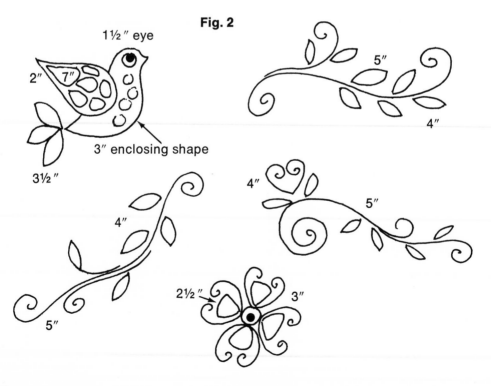

Fig. 2

1½" eye

2" 7"

3" enclosing shape

3½"

4"

5"

5"

4"

4"

5"

2½" 3"

Fig. 3

Pearl

2″

2″

3″

Border design

are best. Arrange larger motifs at the top left corner, smaller motifs at the lower right. If the invitation has straight or cut edges, make a quilled border such as fig. 3 along the parts of the edge that show. If the edges are deckled or cut in interesting shapes, a quilled border is not necessary. Use taste in your arrangement.

If the frame has sufficient depth, place some units over others—flowers over leaves, a wing on top of a bird.

Other sentimental mementos of the occasion, such as a bit of net and a piece of ribbon from the bridal bouquet, should be included. Cut the ribbon into strips (fig. 4) and glue on with the net. A piece of this ribbon, split into $\frac{1}{16}$″ strips, can also be made into a lattice (fig. 5).

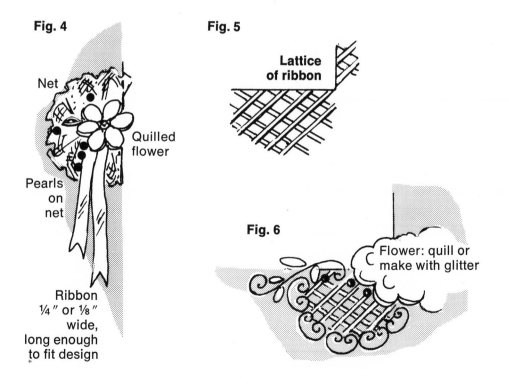

Fig. 4

Net

Quilled flower

Pearls on net

Ribbon ¼″ or ⅛″ wide, long enough to fit design

Fig. 5

Lattice of ribbon

Fig. 6

Flower: quill or make with glitter

Fig. 7

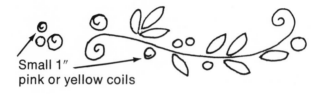

Small 1"
pink or yellow coils

On smaller pieces of tissue, trace from your design the individual units you plan to use (bird, flowers, tendrils). Quill them, using white and pastel colors. Make a lattice and trim it to fit.

When you've finished quilling, assemble the design on the background, using your drawing as a guide for placement. Glue on the lattice, and surround it with quilled scrolls (fig. 6). Glue flowers and tendrils over the scrolls. Glue on net and ribbon (fig. 4) as you glue in quilled units, fitting it around and under the quilling.

Scatter tight, colored coils here and there to complete the design and add extra color (fig. 7). Add pearls, beads, or jewels where you wish; glue them to the quilling or background. When all the glue is dry, replace the board in the frame.

This type of quilling can be used to embellish any printed piece: a favorite saying, a poem, a certificate or any other special award (fig. 8).

Fig. 8

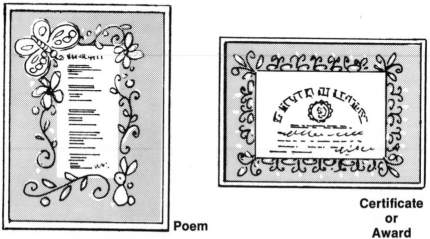

Poem

Certificate
or
Award

VALENTINES

Paper Heart

Here is a simple-to-make valentine that anyone would be proud to present to her love. Children also enjoy making paper valentines; some suggestions for them appear at the end of this section.

Materials needed: ⅛″ white quilling strips and a few ³⁄₁₆″ strips to be sprayed gold; a box with a clear plastic top about 5″ x 6½″ (stationery or notecard box); gift wrap paper; gold edging foil or fabric braid (the stick-on kind is good); gold gift tie cord; red paper; paint; card; gold spray paint; rubber cement.

If the box is too deep, cut it to make a depth of about ¾″. Cover the outside with bright print or foil gift wrap, gluing with rubber cement. Paint the inside of the box, or line it with blue or purple gift wrap, foil, or velour.

Trace the half heart (see fig. 1, next page) on folded paper; turn paper over and trace the other side. Transfer to red paper. Glue paper to cardboard and cut out the heart. Quill the edging as shown, and glue it onto the edge of the heart. Glue gold cord around heart next to the quilled edge. Quill the letters for "LOVE" (fig. 2), and spray them gold. When the paint is dry, cover the surface of the heart with glue and stick on the letters forming the word "LOVE." Glue the complete heart into the bottom of the box (fig. 3). Tape the top on. Glue or stick on trim around the edge on top of the clear plastic to complete the valentine.

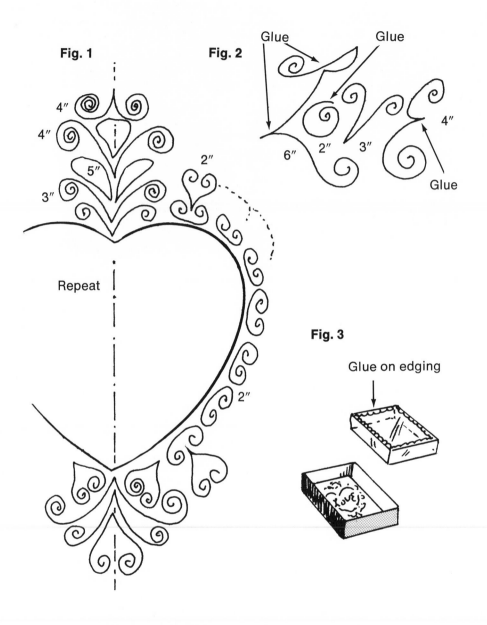

Fig. 1

4″

4″

5″

3″

2″

Repeat

2″

Fig. 2

Glue   Glue

6″   2″   3″   4″

Glue

Fig. 3

Glue on edging

The word "LOVE" could be made for a permanent decoration, if preferred (fig. 4), by mounting it on a 2″ x 4″ piece of card covered with purple or other bright paper or fabric. Quill a simple edge around this panel. Mount it on a 5″ x 6½″ panel of black or dark-stained wood, add a hanger, and hang it on a wall.

Fig. 4

Fig. 5

**Folded
scroll heart**

CHILDREN'S VALENTINES: If a youngster wishes to make this valentine, make the heart twice as big. Make the quilling of ¼″ strips. Mount the finished piece in the cover of a gift box (like a small shirt box); it does not need the transparent covering.

Let children make up their own ideas for quilled valentines to fit into box covers, whatever size they may have. The basic heart scroll (fig. 5) is easy. Fig. 6 shows a few suggested ideas. Combine the quilled shapes with paper lace hearts, gold foil trims, cut paper shapes, or cut or punched-out valentine figures.

Fig. 6

Row of hearts in tie box

Flower of
hearts

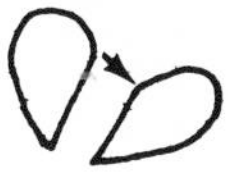

Two pinched coils
glued together.
Mount 3 units on
a ribbon. ➝

Paper lace heart
accentuated with
quillwork

Hearts and flowers, quilled

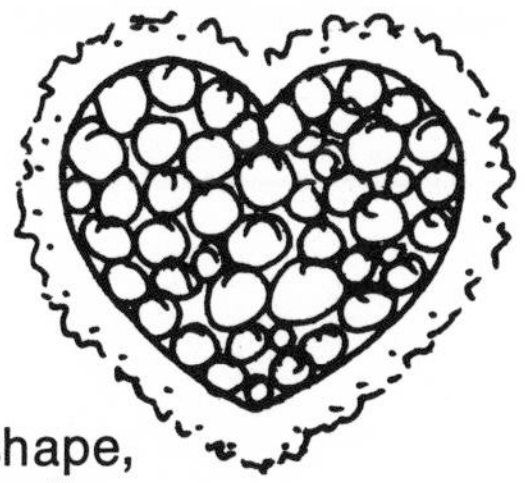

Enclosed shape,
filled with coils
(see animals page 59).
Paste onto lace heart.

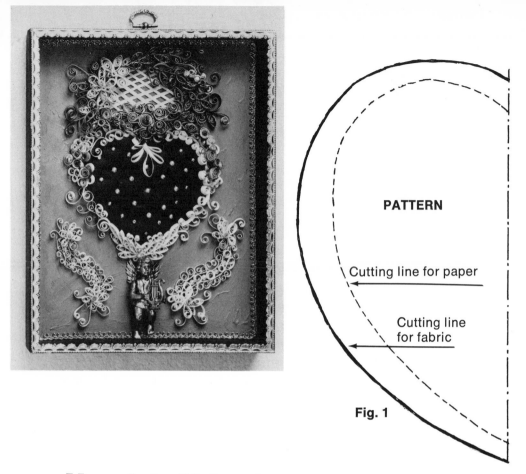

PATTERN

Cutting line for paper

Cutting line
for fabric

Fig. 1

Nostalgic Valentine

This can be a truly magnificent keepsake. An English quillwork decoration for a wax portrait, dating to 1702, inspired this valentine. Gilding and the use of many layers of quilling add to its appeal.

Materials needed: 1/8″ quilling paper in white, muted greens, pink, yellow, tan and gray (1/16″ wide); purchased shadow box about 8″ x 10″, or a homemade one (see page 39); decorative edgings (gold paper or fabric type); piece of red velvet (or red paper); pearls or gold beads; gold paint; decorative hanger; 8″ x 10″ piece of glass or plastic; and a cupid figure if desired.

Paint the inside bottom of the box blue or purple (or cover it with paper). Paint the frame a dark color inside and out.

The heart in center can be simply made of paper. Trace the dotted line (fig. 1), then trace the other half. Cut out the

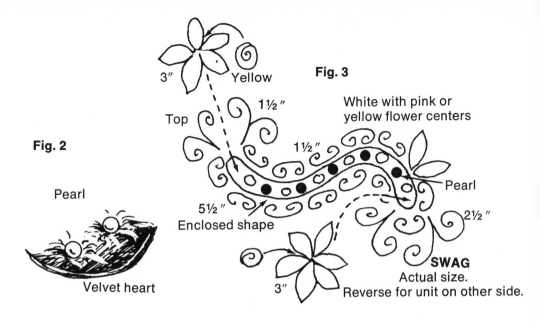

Fig. 3

Fig. 2

Pearl

Top

3" Yellow

1½"

1½"

White with pink or
yellow flower centers

Pearl

5½"
Enclosed shape

2½"

Velvet heart

3"

SWAG
Actual size.
Reverse for unit on other side.

heart. Or make the heart an enclosed shape and fill it with pinched red coils.

For real elegance, use red velvet for the heart. Trace and complete the outline (the solid line in fig. 1). Cut two hearts of velvet. Place the right sides together and sew around the edges, making a ¼" seam. Turn the heart right side out, and stuff, making the center about ¾" thick. Sew the edge closed.

Sew on pearls at intervals. Bring the needle and thread up from back, through the pearl, and straight down again through the fabric. Tie the thread in back firmly, making the velvet puff up around the pearl (fig. 2).

Using white strips quill the two design units for the lower corners, and add flowers with colored centers on top of each (fig. 3). Make a lattice of gray or pink 1/16" wide strips. Make white flowers and leaf swags of green to edge the lattice (fig. 4). Add tan scrolls. Use conical coils in the centers for accents. Glue units on top of the edging of the lattice, building up the design. Glue scrolls onto the top for more dimension. Occasionally, pull a scroll out at an angle (fig. 5). Quill white edging to fit around the heart (fig. 6).

Plan positioning and arrange the quilled units in box, including the figurine (if you are using one). When you are satisfied with the arrangement, glue the heart to the backing. Glue on the quilled units, lattice, and quilled edging for heart, fitting

Fig. 4

PATTERN
actual size

7½" 6" 1¾"

3½"

4"

2½"

5"

4"

5" 20"
conical
coil center

5½" Pinched coils

First layer

2"

White
flowers,
green
tendrils

5"

4"

3"

Flower center
(place on top)

Glue this unit around
conical coils, over
pinched coils

5½"

4"

5¼"

4" 4½"

Second layer

it up and over the edge of the fabric. For the top center of the
heart, make five loops, gluing the ends together (fig. 7). Glue
over heart. Make more tight coils and glue them on top of the
coils at each side of the upper corners of heart border (see
fig. 6). Add more tan scrolls to the decoration above the heart

if needed. Fill in between the heart and lattice with tan coils and scrolls.

For an elegant effect, paint gold on the edges of green and tan coils wherever desired, especially the center unit above the heart. Glue pearls or gold beads in the centers of open coils and between the coils (see dots in fig. 3 and 4).

Glue (or stick on) gold edging where the sides meet the backing (fig. 8). Make sure all the pieces are secure. Have a piece of glass cut to fit the front, or cut a piece of plastic to size. Glue it to the front edges of the shadow box. Glue on gold foil trim, covering the edge, and attach a decorative hanger to the top.

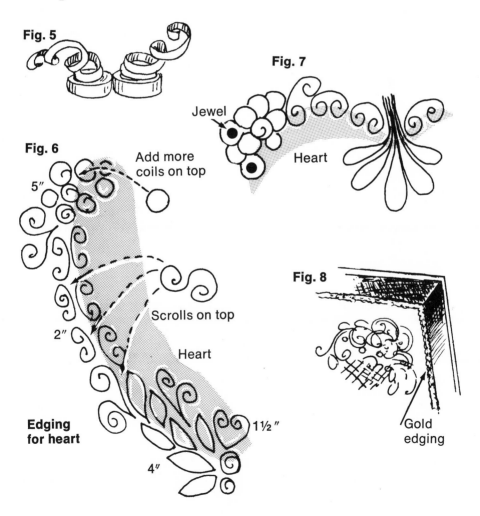

Fig. 5

Fig. 7

Jewel

Heart

Fig. 6

Add more
coils on top

5"

2"

Scrolls on top

Heart

Fig. 8

Edging
for heart

1½"

4"

Gold
edging

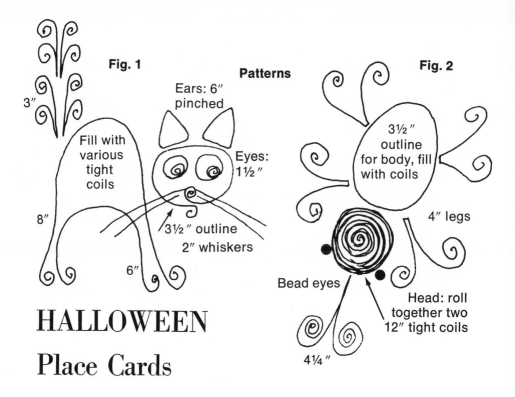

Fig. 1

Patterns

Fig. 2

3″

Ears: 6″ pinched

Fill with various tight coils

Eyes: 1½″

3½″ outline for body, fill with coils

8″

3½″ outline

2″ whiskers

4″ legs

Bead eyes

Head: roll together two 12″ tight coils

6″

4¼″

HALLOWEEN

Place Cards

Preparing for parties can be half the fun. Quilled place cards can be appropriate for either children's or adult parties. Glue a simple flower or bird (page 47) on a card. It will be taken home as a keepsake of a pleasant tea party, a memorable birthday, or any other occasion.

For Halloween, make black cat or spider place cards. *Materials:* For each card; ⅛″ black quilling strips and a 6″ square of orange posterboard or card.

For the cat, trace the design (fig. 1) and quill as indicated. The feet strips go up and around to make an enclosed body shape. Fill the body with tight coils. Glue together curled-end strips to make the tail. Make the head, and glue whiskers on top to make a second layer. For the spider, trace the design and quill as shown (fig. 2).

Fold the orange card in half, glue the cat or spider to the card at one side. If desired, glue on two green beads as eyes. Letter the guest's name onto the place card (fig. 3).

Fig. 3

ree Cross

ee cross that is now part of a museum collection in
Italy, inspired the design for this Easter cross. You can
paper filigree as a freestanding unit, or the cross can be
r hung.

terials needed for the standing cross: ⅛″ white quill-
(some ¼″ wide); five ice cream sticks (craft sticks);
ls on a string and seven pearls about ³⁄₁₆″ to ½″ in
a jewel or other center unit (about ½″ in diameter);
nt. For base: 3″ square piece of 1¼″ thick Styrofoam
from packing can be used); small artificial flowers;
ring about 5″ in diameter.

the ice cream sticks as shown (fig. 1) and glue the cut
her. This will be adequate backing if you plan to hang
unit. When the quilling is done, glue a hanging
eted unit. When the quilling is done, glue a hanging
top stick. If you plan to frame the cross, no wood

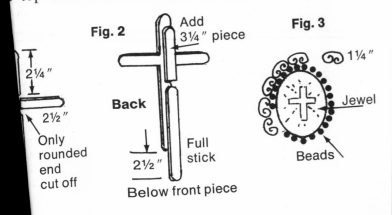

Fig. 2

2¼″

2½″
Only
rounded
end
cut off

Back

Add
3¼″ piece

2½″
Below front piece

Full
stick

Fig. 3

1¼″

Jewel

Beads

EASTER
Egg Fantasy

"Eggers" spend all year long glorifying the noble shape of the egg,
but at Easter, almost everyone tries egg decorating—the more
elaborate the decoration, the better. Paper filigree is ideal egg
ornamentation.

Materials needed: ⅛″ quilling paper in several pastel
colors; large plastic egg about 4″ tall; or egg shape made of
Styrofoam foam (or the plastic egg-shaped case from panty hose);
picture or print; gold cord or ribbon; beads or pearls (molded
on a string); jewels; lightweight card; paint.

For the stand, cut a piece of card 5½″ x ½″. Curve it
around and glue. Quill decorations, and glue on the base (fig. 1).
When the glue is dry, spray-paint gold. Keep setting the egg into
the stand as you work to make sure the quilling does not extend
too far down.

Paint the egg shape (or spray-paint, if it is plastic). Trace
oval shown (fig. 2). Select a suitable picture for the center of
the design from a magazine, brochure, or greeting card. Lay the
tracing over it to determine the proper size picture. Cut the picture out. If desired, cut a similar picture for the other side of
the egg.

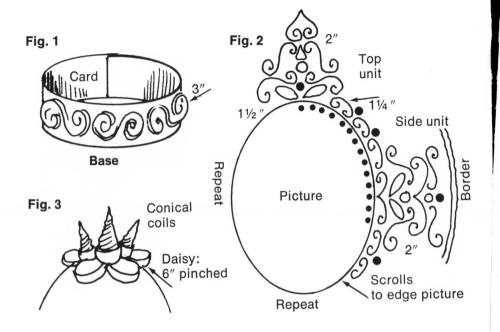

Fig. 1

Card

3″

Base

Fig. 2

2″

Top unit

1¼″

1½″

Side unit

Border

Repeat

Picture

Fig. 3

Conical coils

Daisy: 6″ pinched

2″

Scrolls to edge picture

Repeat

Glue the pictures on egg. If wrinkles occur along the edges, press them out with a slightly damp sponge (*don't rub*). Keep smoothing until the glue sets. Glue a row of tiny pearls at the edge of the picture.

Decide on a color scheme, such as lavender and green with small touches of blue. If you are using a plastic egg that comes in two parts, glue a color strip around the center to hide and hold the joining.

Place the drawing of the oval under the waxed paper and quill four units for the top, bottom, and sides (fig. 2). Glue each unit to the egg against the row of pearls, holding the quilling with masking tape while drying. Press down frequently to help the quilling curve onto the egg surface. Fill in between with as many scrolls as necessary to complete the frame and edge picture (fig. 2).

Make a daisy of five pinched coils. Glue them to a conical coil, then to the top of the egg (fig. 3). Add a small conical coil to each side of the flower.

Quill two side border units (fig. 4), gluing cord or beads along the edges, and glue the borders to egg. Quill four leaf swags (fig. 5). Glue them in the open areas between the frame

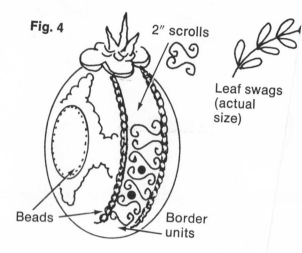

Fig. 4

2″ scrolls

Leaf swags (actual size)

Beads

Border units

and border. Make extra scrolls to glu
are needed to enhance the design. Re

For a jeweled treasure look,
beads on the coils or between quilli
angles to the surface to add dimen
rated egg to the stand to complete.

OTHER EGG IDEAS: Decorate
cate. For a blown egg, color, make
ing around the opening. Frame the
(fig. 7) and quill a design for the
with clear nail polish for strength
(many types are available from c
to the top of the egg. Make quil
for inside the egg, or set a tiny

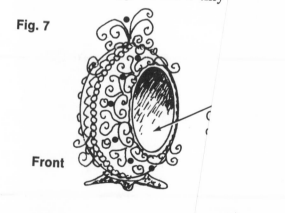

Fig. 7

Front

Fili

A filigr
Abruzzi
make the
framed

M
ing pape
tiny pear
diameter:
white pai
(a corner
or candle

Cut
ends toget
the compl
cord to th

Fig. 1

2½″

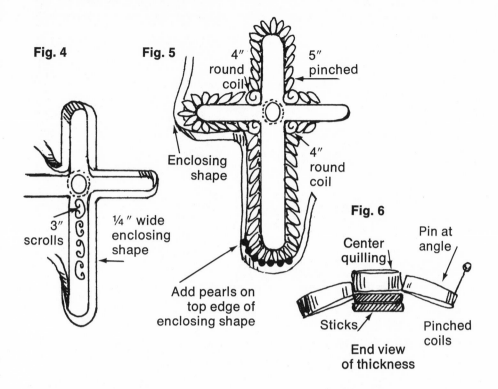

Fig. 4

3" scrolls

¼" wide enclosing shape

Fig. 5

4" round coil

5" pinched

Enclosing shape

4" round coil

Add pearls on top edge of enclosing shape

Fig. 6

Center quilling

Pin at angle

Sticks

Pinched coils

End view of thickness

backing is necessary; just glue the completed quilling to a dark background.

For a standing unit, glue two more sticks onto the back (fig. 2), allowing stick to project below so that it can be inserted in a base later. Paint the sticks white.

Glue on a center decoration: a medallion, small picture, jewel, or tight lavender coil. The jewel used in the cross shown has a tiny cross within it (available in craft shops). Surround the jewel with double scrolls (fig. 3). Glue a row of tiny beads or pearls over scrolls around the edge of the jewel.

Make enclosed shapes around the arms of the cross, gluing ¼" strips along the edges of sticks (fig. 4), and making ⅛" depth in front for quillwork. Fill enclosed shapes with double scrolls, facing in alternate directions.

Make a quantity of 5" double pinched coils. Lay the cross on the quilling board and glue a round coil at each intersection. Glue pinched coils to the arms, angling as shown (fig. 5). Because of the sticks' thickness, the coils will tilt down slightly as the outer ends are pinned to the board (fig. 6). This adds a dimensional

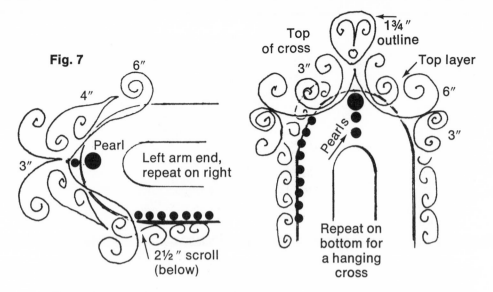

Fig. 7

6"

4"

3"

Pearl

Left arm end,
repeat on right

2½" scroll
(below)

Top
of cross

1¾"
outline

3"

Top layer

6"

3"

Pearls

Repeat on
bottom for
a hanging
cross

effect. As you glue on the coils, add an ⅛" wide enclosing shape around all outside edges (see fig. 5). If desired, glue tiny beads or strung pearls along the top edge of this enclosing strip.

Now embellish the cross with as many scrolls as desired along the outside edges and at the tips (fig. 7). Add quilled motifs at the intersections, gluing them over pinched coils for more dimensions (fig. 8). Glue larger pearls at tips and intersections (see fig. 7 and 8). If the cross is to be hung or framed, repeat the top quilling motifs at the bottom also.

For the base to hold a standing unit, glue strings of beads around the 3" square piece or add a quilled design if desired (fig. 9). Make a ⅜" slit in the center of the base to insert the end of the stick. Place a small candle ring on top of the base, then insert the stick through the middle of the ring and into the base. Glue the end of the stick, if necessary, to hold the cross steady.

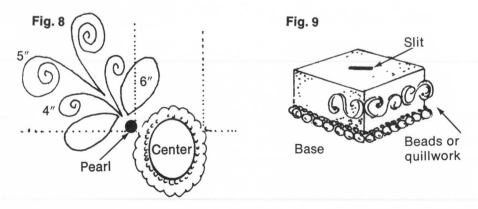

Fig. 8

5"

6"

4"

Pearl

Center

Fig. 9

Slit

Base

Beads or
quillwork

CHRISTMAS

Tree Ornaments

Any small quilled frame design can be adapted to make Christmas tree ornaments. Thin bracelets, toothpicks, or straws can add body and strength. Here are some suggestions.

Materials needed: ⅛″ quilling strips; old Christmas cards; gold spray; jewels; beads or other sparkly trims. For hanging cords, use very fine gold thread or nylon line.

FRAMED SCENE: Select an oval or round picture from a used Christmas card. Draw the outline of the shape on a piece of paper. Mount the picture on a piece of decorative card so the back of the ornament is also attractive. Cut out. Curl the ends of a colored strip. Glue it around edge, gluing curls to the back as shown (fig. 1). Make the edge even with the front. Turn over.

Place drawn shape under the waxed paper, make a frame

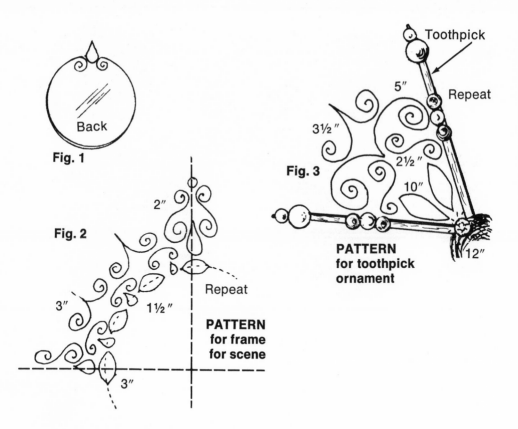

Fig. 1

Back

Fig. 2

2"

3"

1½"

3"

Repeat

PATTERN
for frame
for scene

Fig. 3

Toothpick

5"

Repeat

3½"

2½"

10"

12"

PATTERN
for toothpick
ornament

of tight coils and scrolls. Fig. 2 is a suggestion for one-quarter of the frame. Make repeats between center points, adding or eliminating scrolls as needed to fit your picture. Make quilling in red and green or any color combination that compliments the picture, or spray the frame gold. Glue the frame around the picture, and tie on a hanging line.

TOOTHPICK ORNAMENT: For the center, make a firm tight 12" coil of ¼" wide strip. Place five flat toothpicks at approximately equal distances apart. Glue the tips to the center coil. Quill five units (fig. 3); glue them between the toothpicks. When the glue is dry, spray the ornament gold. Add glue to the tips of each toothpick, and slide two ½" or ⅜" diameter beads on each. Glue bright-colored seed beads or small jewels along the the toothpicks and to spots in the quilling to add sparkle. Make a colored conical coil (see page 33). Glue it to the center (fig. 4), and repeat on other side. Tie on a hanging cord.

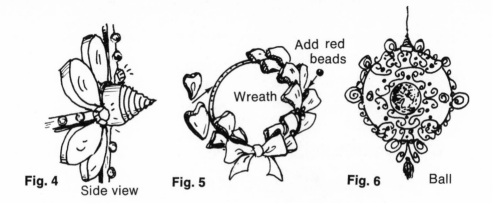

Fig. 4 Side view

Add red beads

Wreath

Fig. 5

Fig. 6 Ball

BRACELET AND OTHER ORNAMENTS: Bracelets are a good size for ornaments (see page 54) and they give strength to the quilling. Quill a scrolled frame, glue it to the outside of a bracelet, and hang an ornament inside.

Make a wreath by gluing triple pinched coils to either side of a bracelet. Add red beads and a bow (fig. 5).

Make unique boutique balls with quilled trim. Decorate a satin or Styrofoam ball using methods and designs similar to those used on the eggs (see page 96). Add jewels or other holiday trims, beads or a tassel at the bottom (fig. 6).

The possibilities for quilled ornaments are numerous. Embed quilling to make 3″ transparent disks (see page 74). Or glue a quilled bird to a tiny clothespin (fig. 7), and clip to a branch. Use your ingenuity to adapt quilling to holiday decorations.

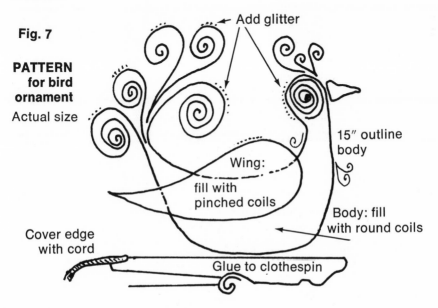

Fig. 7

← Add glitter

PATTERN for bird ornament

Actual size

15″ outline body

Wing: fill with pinched coils

Body: fill with round coils

Cover edge with cord

Glue to clothespin

Filigree Crèche Setting

European cathedrals of the seventeenth century were lavished with paintings, carvings, sculpture, and gold filigree. When a poor person wished to make a religious article, he found quillwork could imitate some of the splendor of the cathedrals.

Quill an ornate setting for the tiny plastic Nativity figures that can be purchased in craft and variety stores. The instructions given here will fit a set of ten figures, the tallest about 1½″ high. If the figures you have are larger, make the base wider and the backing taller. Tiny hand-carved figures or figurines of fine materials can be used instead.

Materials needed: ⅛″ quilling strips (to spray gold); cardboard; gold card backing (from greeting cards); embossed gold foil edging (from a craft store); gift wrap or other decorative papers; white soda straws; rubber cement; three straight pins. For base: Cut a piece of ⅜″ thick balsa wood about 1″ x 6″ or whatever size needed to fit figures.

For the back, trace half the outline (fig. 1), fold the paper and draw the other half, or draw the size needed. Cut out of heavy card or foam core board. Choose a paper (foil, velour, or a mottled gift wrap) for the background of the figures with a color and texture that compliments but does not overwhelm the small figures. Set the base against the backing, and position the figures to check the effect and plan the arrangement.

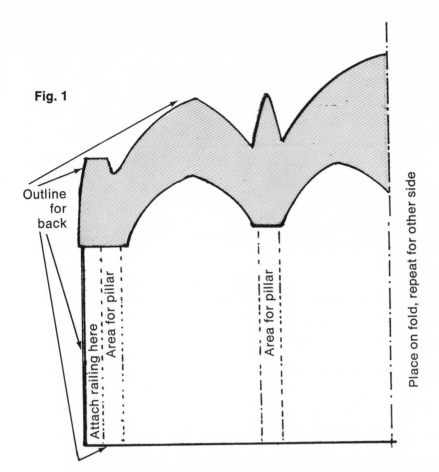

Fig. 1

Outline for back

Attach railing here

Area for pillar

Area for pillar

Place on fold, repeat for other side

Attach paper to the back panel with rubber cement and trim the edges even. Cover the base with a wood-grain or marble stick-on vinyl (or paint it brown). Cut the piece of paper at least ¾″ larger all around than the base. Glue (or stick onto) base. Cut the corners (fig. 2), fold them around, and glue.

To attach the back, push or nail three straight pins (fig. 3) up through the base. Start each hole with an awl. Add glue to the bottom edge of the back and push it down onto the base. Glue a ⅛″ strip of gold edging over the joining in front (fig. 4).

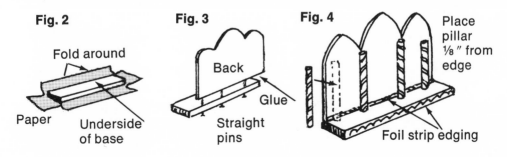

Fig. 2

Fold around

Paper

Underside of base

Fig. 3

Back

Glue

Straight pins

Fig. 4

Place pillar ⅛″ from edge

Foil strip edging

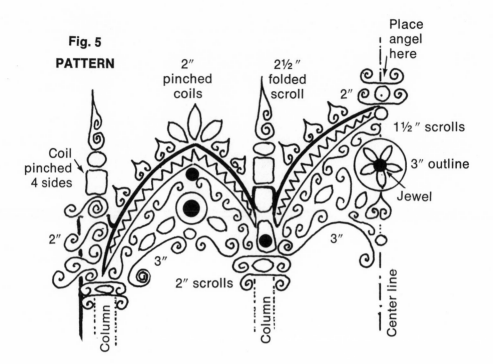

Fig. 5
PATTERN

2" pinched coils

2½" folded scroll

Place angel here

2"

Coil pinched 4 sides

1½" scrolls

3" outline

Jewel

2"

3"

Column

2" scrolls

Column

Center line

3"

For pillars, cut straws: two pieces 1¾" and two pieces 2¼" long (or the size needed to fit the height you are using). For spiral trimming, use ⅛" wide (or less) gold foil strips or narrow gold ribbon. Cover both straw and trimming with rubber cement. When the cement is dry, wind the trimming around the straw, making an even spiral. Repeat, reversing the direction of spiral on two of the straws (fig. 4). Rub off excess cement. Glue the pillars into position. Glue ⅜" decorative gold foil edging around the front and sides of the base as shown.

Trace the top shape (shaded area in fig. 1), then draw the other half. Cut the shape out of gold card. Glue it to the backing, aligning top edges.

Trace the quilling design for the top (fig. 5) and complete the other half. Place the design under waxed paper and quill shapes suggested. Make enclosed shapes first, add scrolls, coils, and crimping. Make scrolls to fit the top of pillars.

If your Nativity set includes an angel, make a proper space for her to stand on (or against) at the center top. Make a tight coil and set it horizontally, then glue it to the top center of the scroll. If no angel is included, quill pinched shape decorations similar to the side units.

Glue about ten tight coil stilts behind the quilling to hold it slightly away from the background. Glue a stilt behind each scroll that will rest on a pillar. Trace railing shape (fig. 6), and quill two. When the quilling is dry, lift it off board and spray all units gold.

After the paint dries, position the quilling, aligning it to the top. Glue stilts to the backing, quilling to the top of the pillars. Glue a railing at each end (fig. 7).

Glue all figures in position as planned. Glue on gold edging or ribbon to cover any exposed edges of card (fig. 7). Glue paper or gold card to the back and under the base. To further embellish, add flat-back jewels, beads, gold filigree ornaments (fig. 8), or other decorations on the quilling.

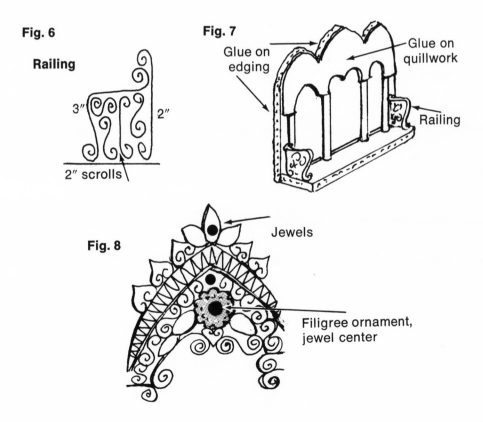

Fig. 6

Railing

3"   2"

2" scrolls

Fig. 7

Glue on edging

Glue on quillwork

Railing

Fig. 8

Jewels

Filigree ornament, jewel center

Skating Santa

Here is a good family or schoolroom project. Various sections of this Santa (cuff, hat, package, etc.) could be made by different people, then the pieces assembled.

Materials needed: ⅜″ white quilling strips (plus some gray and red ones; corrugated card; gift wrap paper; rubber cement; pink, white, black, red paper (or red could be fabric). For backing to mount Santa on, cut a piece of corrugated card 15″ x 20″.

Enlarge the pattern on page 110, as indicated. On pieces of paper, trace the separate sections of the enlarged drawing. Make one section at a time. Trace on white paper and cut out the hat edge, beard shape, cuffs, and jacket trim. Make medium loose coils of white 4″ strips. Glue coils along the edge of each white piece (except the beard, which is done later). When the edge coils are firm, fill the center area with coils (fig. 1).

Fig. 1

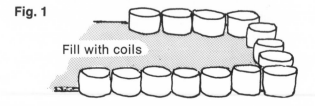

Fill with coils

Trace the suit, hat, and legs (gray areas on the pattern). Cut these shapes out of corrugated card. Cover the suit, hat, and upper legs with red paper, crepe paper, or fabric, allowing extra to fold around any edge which will show (fig. 2). Add glue, fold around, cut notches to eliminate any excess, and glue to back. Cover the boot area on each leg with black paper, allowing the paper to fold around to the back where necessary.

Cut the face out of pink paper, the mittens from a bright-colored card or fabric. Cut package of corrugated board, and cover with a bright patterned gift wrap paper, folding around sides so that the corrugated edges are covered.

For covering the background use an unpatterned gift wrap paper (such as green foil). Cut a piece 2″ larger all around. Cover the board and back of paper with rubber cement. When dry, lay the board on the paper, wrap the paper around edge, and glue the paper onto the back. Smooth the surface in front.

Now assemble the units. Lightly trace the general outline of Santa in position on the board. Glue all units in place, gluing the body first.

For the beard, glue a white strip around the beard area, making an enclosed shape. Quill some "S" curves of 3½″ white strips. Glue scrolls over the enclosed area in a random pattern to look like a swirly beard.

Fig. 2

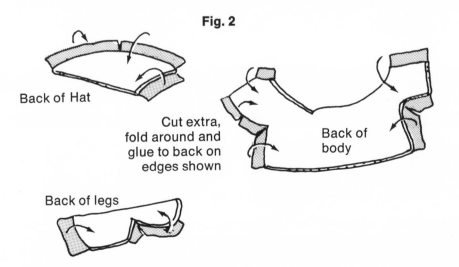

Back of Hat

Cut extra,
fold around and
glue to back on
edges shown

Back of
body

Back of legs

For the face, roll a 5″ very tight black coil for each eye, and a 12″ tight red coil for nose. Make a pinched 2½″ red coil for the mouth. For the mustache, make two white 12″ open coils, pinch on one end, and shape them to fit the outline. Glue face units into position, holding pieces with pins stuck into the backing until the glue sets.

For each skate, make scrolls shown of gray paper. Add glue to the edges and glue them in position, holding with pins. Make white coils for the tip of the cap, and quill bright colors for the package bow. Glue in position.

This Santa could be placed in a frame or tacked on a bulletin board or door for the holidays.

Pattern

8″

Fill with coils

Fill with 3½″ scrolls

12″

12″

Fill with coils

Fill with coils

Fill with coils

4½″

7″

SANTA PATTERN

Draw ¼″ grid over picture. On a 15″ × 20″ piece of paper, draw 1″ squares. Enlarge the pattern.

Heirloom Tree Wall Plaque

At Christmas time, nothing is too ornate. Quilled creations can be lavished with all kinds of sparkles, re-creating the elegant embellishments of seventeenth-century quilling. The details for this holiday tree were taken from an old sconce. Make the basic swags and flowers, then fill in as little or as much as you like. If you'd prefer an heirloom wall piece that is not seasonal, just make a triangle (without the trunk area) and quill designs with a different color scheme.

   Materials needed for tree: ¼″ strips in green, red, blue, and a color to be sprayed gold. Also needed: corrugated board (or foam core board); two yardsticks; paint; ½ yard of fabric (or paper) for background; green and red card or paper; ¼″ finishing nails; small pinecones about ½″ diameter. For flowers: gold wire; cardboard; paint; and glitter (see page 32). Also add old jewelry; earrings, beads, and jewels.

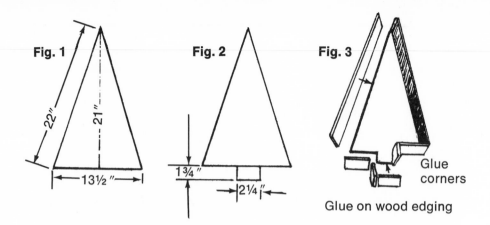

Fig. 1

22"

21"

13½"

Fig. 2

1¾"

2¼"

Fig. 3

Glue corners

Glue on wood edging

To make the background, draw an isosceles triangle of the size shown (fig. 1) on corrugated card. For the trunk, add a rectangle (fig. 2). Cut out the shape. Cover with dark brown or black paper or fabric, felt or velvet, cut 1" larger all around. Add glue. Stick the fabric on, fold it around the shape, and glue it in back.

For the frame, measure and cut yardsticks (or ⅛" x 1" wooden strips) to fit each edge of the cut shape (seven pieces). Paint the wood dark green and antique it if desired. Add glue to the edges of the cardboard. Nail and glue on the strips (fig. 3), gluing the corners together where they meet. When the glue is dry, fill the corners with plastic wood if necessary. Sand, and touch up the paint. Your tree-shaped shadow box is now complete.

For quilling, trace the outlines of the swag shapes (fig. 4),

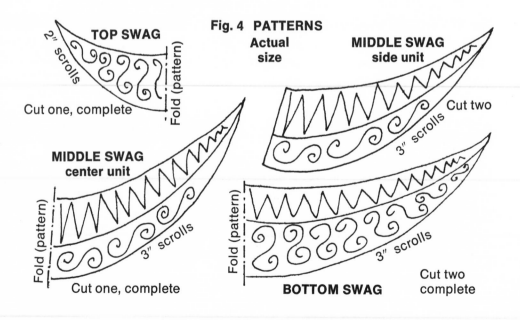

2" scrolls

TOP SWAG

Fold (pattern)

Cut one, complete

Fig. 4 PATTERNS
Actual size

MIDDLE SWAG
side unit

3" scrolls

Cut two

MIDDLE SWAG
center unit

Fold (pattern)

3" scrolls

Cut one, complete

Fold (pattern)

3" scrolls

Cut two
complete

BOTTOM SWAG

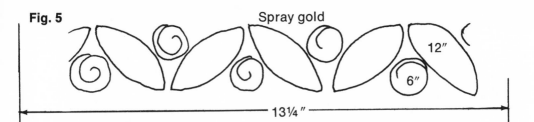

Fig. 5

Spray gold

12"

6"

13¼"

completing the other half where indicated. Cut out of red paper
or card the number of swags indicated. Place each shape under the
waxed paper and make the enclosed shapes. Fill them with crimping and "S" curves as indicated.

For the bottom of the tree, make a row 13¼" long, alternat-
ing pinched and tight coils (fig. 5). For the trunk, quill an enclosed
section 2⅛" x 1", and fill it with tight coils.

Trace the outline of the vase shape (fig. 6), make an enclosed shape and fill it with coils. Glue three pinched coils to a
center coil (fig. 7), and add scrolls.

When the glue is dry, spray-paint gold all the quilling completed so far. When the paint is dry, glue the quilled gold swags to
the flat red swag shapes (from fig. 4).

Trace the heavy outline of the gray shape in fig. 8 on
paper. Fold the paper and draw the other half. Transfer the design to green paper or card and cut it out. Place it on top of the
quilling board.

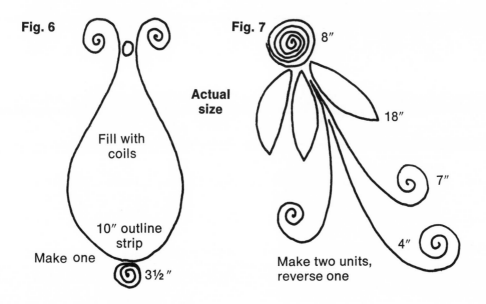

Fig. 6

Fill with
coils

Actual
size

10" outline
strip

Make one

3½"

Fig. 7

8"

18"

7"

4"

Make two units,
reverse one

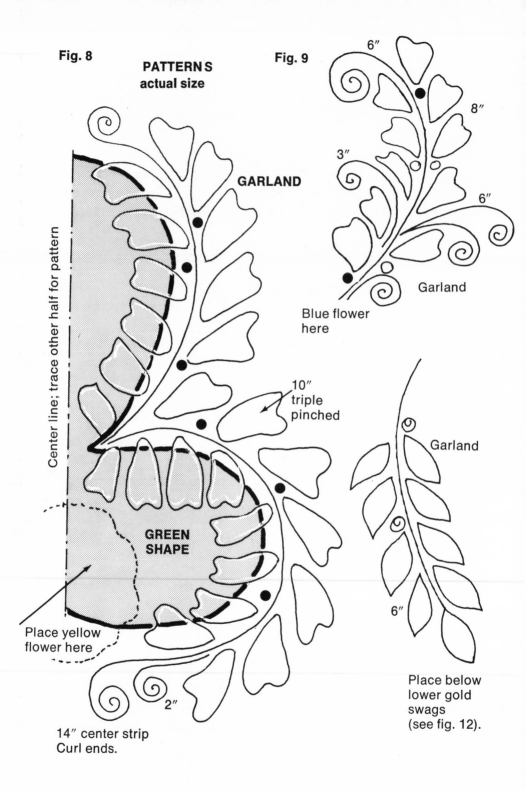

Fig. 8

PATTERNS actual size

Fig. 9

GARLAND

Center line; trace other half for pattern

6"

8"

3"

6"

Garland

Blue flower here

10" triple pinched

Garland

GREEN SHAPE

Place yellow flower here

6"

Place below lower gold swags (see fig. 12).

2"

14" center strip Curl ends.

For green quilling, try to use several shades of green, since variations give the finished piece a more intriguing look. Paint green paper with various streaks of deeper greens before cutting the strips. Make four green garlands of triple pinched coils. Glue them to the flat green shape so that the center strip of the garland is about ¼" outside the edge of the flat shape (fig. 8). Quill other green garlands (fig. 9) and tendrils as shown. Make a 13½" strip of green scrolls.

Now make the flowers. Trace petal shapes (fig. 10) and cut them out of cardboard, making the number indicated of each size. Paint each shape the color shown, keeping the colors subtle for an antique effect. Add glue and transparent glitter. Edge each petal with wire coils (see page 32) of the size indicated in fig. 10. For centers, make tight coils: using 12" for red and yellow flowers, 10" for the small red flower center. For the large blue flower, coil two 12" strips (blue and yellow) together to make a coil about ¾" in diameter. Assemble each flower with a temporary collar gluing the petals to a center coil (fig. 11).

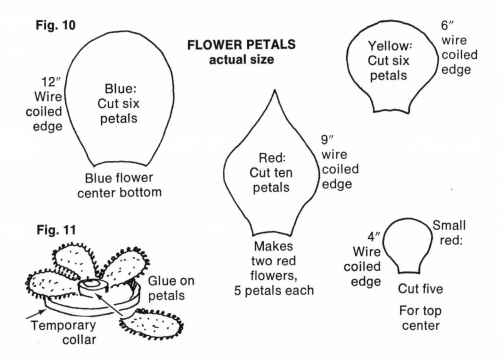

Fig. 10

FLOWER PETALS
actual size

12"
Wire
coiled
edge

Blue:
Cut six
petals

Blue flower
center bottom

Yellow:
Cut six
petals

6"
wire
coiled
edge

Red:
Cut ten
petals

9"
wire
coiled
edge

Makes
two red
flowers,
5 petals each

4"
Wire
coiled
edge

Small
red:

Cut five

For top
center

Fig. 11

Glue on
petals

Temporary
collar

You now have enough pieces to start assembling the tree. Fig. 12 is a general idea for arrangement. Lay in all the quilled units and shift them until they are attractive within the frame. Pick up each piece, add glue, and attach it to the backing.

Now fill in as much extra detail as you like. A row of pinecones can fill the trunk around the gold area and between the garland edge and the area around the conical coils on the flat green shape. Place cones in various spots under swags and along edges.

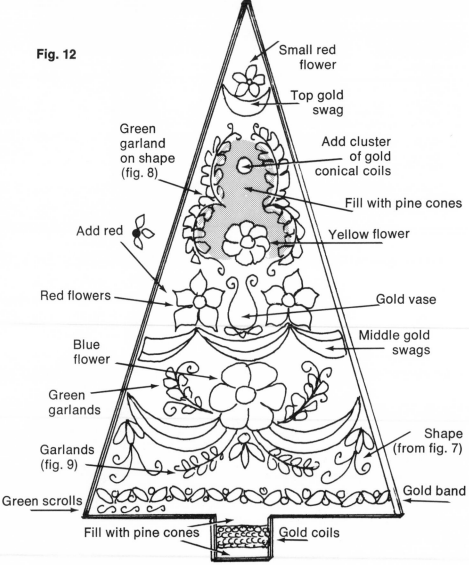

Fig. 12

Small red flower

Top gold swag

Green garland on shape (fig. 8)

Add cluster of gold conical coils

Fill with pine cones

Add red

Yellow flower

Red flowers

Gold vase

Blue flower

Middle gold swags

Green garlands

Garlands (fig. 9)

Shape (from fig. 7)

Green scrolls

Gold band

Fill with pine cones

Gold coils

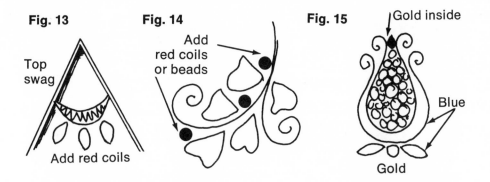

Fig. 13

Top swag

Add red coils

Fig. 14

Add red coils or beads

Fig. 15

Gold inside

Blue

Gold

Quill red loops and coils, and scatter them about to add color (fig. 13 and 14). Add a blue coil around the vase shape in the center (fig. 15). Add scrolls or conical coils around flower centers, a conical coil cluster in center of green shape.

Set up the tree and look at it. Does it look empty in spots? Add colored coils or scrolls where needed. Add some blue scrolls between gold ones at bottom (fig. 16), some blue ones at the edges of the large red flowers (fig. 17). Also add jewels and jewelry. An old earring drop (its mate long lost) might fit into the top peak. Other earrings (especially the plastic holiday type) can add a touch of gold or color by the flowers or below swags. Glue stilts onto earrings, if necessary, to make them sit properly. Use your judgment in choosing color and shapes for fillers and accents.

Glue a hanger on at top, in back. You have created a treasured heirloom for the holidays.

Fig. 16

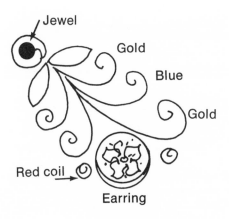

Jewel

Gold

Blue

Gold

Red coil

Earring

Fig. 17

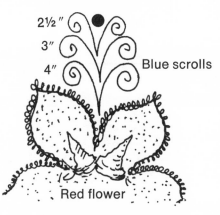

2½"

3"

4"

Blue scrolls

Red flower

Sources of Inspiration

Once you become proficient in handling quilling and following a pattern, you will want to create your own designs. Start by curling some scrolls and coils and see what develops when they are arranged together. For a repeat design, graph paper is helpful in spacing the design. Lay tracing paper over graph paper and draw in motifs.

Most of the projects in this book were inspired either by antique quilled units or classic ornamentations of various other materials. Try sketching designs you see in museums, and looking in art books. Sources of design can be found in European filigrees, scrolled motifs of ironwork, seventeenth-century ornamentations of furniture and bric-a-brac. Cast-gold African work, filigree of the Near East, antique jewelry—the sources of inspiration are endless. Keep in mind shapes that are possible with quilling, then draw a design.

On the following pages are examples in various materials for adapting to quilling, with some examples of adaptations.

GOLD AND SILVER FILIGREE: By the time of the Renaissance in Europe, filigree of precious metals was a highly developed art, embellishing religious articles as well as trinkets. Just as paper filigree was probably invented to allow the poor to create some of this ornate decoration, undoubtedly the first quillwork was an exact copy of a gold or silver filigree piece.

Over the centuries, quillwork developed its own style, but fine examples of filigree can still be excellent sources of ideas for your quillwork designs.

The handle of this nineteenth century spoon of silver filigree could inspire a design for jewelry.

The old engraving (left) shows the silver filigree top of an antique card box. The photograph (above) shows an adaptation of the design. The wooden box was painted black, the design quilled in white.

Many miniature silver filigree items such as this birdcage (and sled, next page) were made by European craftsmen about 1675-1700. A birdcage can be an attractive motif.

Make one as a design (flat), and mount it on a plaque with colorful quilled flowers around the base. Or make it half round for a shadow box. To make a dimensional filigree object, shape a piece of Styrofoam, cover it with plastic film and glue your quilling together, shaping it around on the form. When the object is complete, lift it off and mount it.

A gold filigree antique card box is shown above. Note how the larger swirls are filled with shapes similar to elongated tight pinched coils.

The miniature sled (below) of silver filigree is a charming example of seventeenth century work. It could be recreated in quillwork for a holiday centerpiece. Draw shapes for sides, center and runners. Quill each unit and accent with gold cord or wire. Cut red card shapes for seat and sides. Glue quilling over the red sides and glue them to the seat to form a sled shape.

DECORATIVE IRONWORK: It may seem strange that something as heavy as ironwork could inspire as delicate a craft as paper filigree, but intricate designs were worked in wrought iron, especially by the sixteenth century when scrollwork was so popular. Gates and fences, as well as trivets, keys, chandeliers and other household items were also made of iron. Antique buttons, buckles, boxes and other containers, even pieces of jewelry, were crafted of iron or worked steel. Look in books on this subject; these designs can often inspire quillwork. Wrought iron fences, gates, grills and balconies can also inspire you. If you see an ornate example of wrought iron, take a snapshot. Some part of its scrollwork may get you started on a new quillwork idea.

To the right is a copy of an English chapel door of the thirteenth century showing decorative ironwork hinges.

Shown above is a seven-teeth century gridiron of wrought iron.

COLONIAL QUILLWORK: Inspirations can come from many sources, but you cannot truly appreciate the possibilities of quillwork until you have looked closely at an antique piece. Photography just cannot convey its depth and intricacy. Examples are shown on the title page, in the first chapter and on the following pages. Do try to see a piece for yourself—check your museums and colonial restorations. When you find an authentic piece, look at it from different angles, try to analyze the various elements and materials that were used. Ask yourself—what does each element do to create the intriguing effect?

Of course modern quilling can't be that intricate—it doesn't suit our way of life—but the elements of an old piece can be simplified and redesigned to make units that have the same fascination, yet are appropriate in our homes today.

On the right is a large colonial sconce with peacocks on either side of the base unit. Wax lambs are interspersed in the design. Sparkled flowers with silver wire edges, conical coil clusters, shells, coral and many other elements combine to create the total effect of this piece by Eunice Deering. Inspired by the designs that appear in many such sconces, a composition was made to fit an oval frame (left). A simplified vase holds a few glittered flowers. Conical coil clusters, scrolls, quilled flowers and tiny shells complete the arrangement. Any of the many elements of the complex colonial pieces can start you on your own quilling designs.

Above is the center top detail of the mirror frame shown on the title page. The house is of mosaic coils with filigree balcony; the windows are mica. Crushed red shells are sprinkled on the figure. Trees of fluted paper have brown seeds glued between the branches.

BORDERS AND DESIGNS: Printed borders, corners and designs appear daily in magazines, papers, advertising. Many are suitable to inspire quilled motifs. However, unless you are making many layers, avoid those motifs with lines and scrolls that cross each other. Below and on the next pages are a few that might give you some ideas.

Creating your own quillwork ideas and designs is the ultimate in enjoyment of this fascinating craft.

Craft Suppliers

THE FIRESIDE SHOPPER, Route 2, Gerald, Mo. 63037

QUILLING BEE ENTERPRISES, 4004 Fairway Court, Arlington, Texas 76013

TREE TOYS, P.O. Box 492, Hinsdale, Ill. 60521
- *All carry quilling strips (Tree Toys carries gilt-edge strips); send a stamped, self-addressed envelope for price lists.*

FLORIDA SUPPLY HOUSE, INC., P.O. Box 847, Bradenton, Fla. 33506
- *In addition to quilling strips: jewelry findings, colonial head medallions, jewels, beading wire, and glue.*

HOLIDAY HANDICRAFTS, INC., Winsted, Conn. 06098
- *Resin casting kits, jewelry findings, trims, gold foil edgings, small figures*

LEE WARDS, 1200 St. Charles St., Elgin, Ill. 60120
- *In addition to quilling strips (5/32" wide) and kits: resin casting kits, glitter, edgings, beading wire, jewelry findings, shadow boxes and domed frames; request a free catalogue.*

THE O-P CRAFT CO., INC., 425 Warren St., Sandusky, Ohio 44870
- *Boxes, plaques, shadow boxes, domes and foil edgings*

Index